Praise for *Love and Intuition*

"Sherrie Dillard gives us an invaluable gift that will last a lifetime. She teaches us how to connect to our deepest and most meaningful selves; in doing so, we find true love within. And once we learn to love ourselves, we can attract anything and anyone our heart desires!"

> —Richard E. Zimmerman, spiritual-wealth teacher and
> co-founder of the Alchemy Centre in London

"Connecting love, psi, and passion, psychic author Sherrie Dillard offers invaluable tips on how to develop long-lasting, nurturing relationships by creating true connections—all while discovering the intuitive path to loving yourself, the greatest relationship of all."

> —Kala Ambrose, author of *9 Life Altering Lessons*,
> host of the "Explore Your Spirit with Kala" show,
> and national metaphysical spirituality writer
> for Examiner.com

"This book is truly a gift, brimming with deep insight and practical suggestions, and Ms. Dillard's selfless intention to truly assist her readers is implicit throughout. She realizes that intuition is not just for fortune-telling, but also for unfolding, healing, and allowing the full expression of self. *Love and Intuition* takes the reader on a journey for doing just that. I heartily recommend reading it!"

> —Diane Brandon, integrative intuitive counselor and host of
> "Vibrantly Green with Diane Brandon" on Ecology.com and
> "Vibrant Living" on Webtalkradio.net

"*Love and Intuition* is a masterfully written book that guides the reader on a journey through the intuitive world. There is a passion in this book that stimulates readers to have a greater, deliberate intuitive understanding of their relationships. *Love and Intuition* will resonate with individuals seeking to take an expanded inner understanding out into the world to create more meaningful and loving relationships."

—Bernie Ashman, author of *SignMates*

"This is far more than a book about how to use your intuition to find meaningful intimacy. What impressed me even more was how Sherrie Dillard demonstrates the natural teamwork between human affection and psychic sensitivity. This synergy not only deepens love, but also keeps intuition free of ego's distorting demons. I heartily recommend this worthy follow-up to her earlier book *Discover Your Psychic Type*."

—Steven Forrest, author of *The Inner Sky*

"If there were an owner's manual on love, this would be it. Dillard understands and effectively teaches that keen insight into ourselves opens intuition, that soulful awareness builds confidence, and that confidence attracts the most desired love."

—S. Kelley Harrell, shaman and author of
Gift of the Dreamtime

"Sherrie's book is a must read for anyone who has struggled with love. More importantly, it is a vital addition to the bookshelves of anyone looking to deepen their own spiritual experience and connection."

—Allison Agius, author of *Hidden Secrets, Buried Treasure*

LOVE
and
INTUITION

About the Author

For over twenty years, Sherrie Dillard, M.Div., has been a New Thought pastoral counselor, as well as a psychic, medium, and teacher with an international client base. Her passion and enthusiasm for the fusion of intuition, spirituality, and conscious self-growth have made her a popular speaker at conferences and retreats.

Dillard has taught classes and workshops, both nationally and internationally, on the practical, spiritual, and life-enhancing aspects of intuition development.

Please visit her website at www.sherriedillard.com.

To Write to the Author

If you wish to contact the author or would like more information about this book, please write to the author in care of Llewellyn Worldwide Ltd. and we will forward your request. Both the author and publisher appreciate hearing from you and learning of your enjoyment of this book and how it has helped you. Llewellyn Worldwide Ltd. cannot guarantee that every letter written to the author can be answered, but all will be forwarded. Please write to:

Sherrie Dillard
℅ Llewellyn Worldwide Ltd.
2143 Wooddale Drive
Woodbury, MN 55125-2989

Please enclose a self-addressed stamped envelope for reply,
or $1.00 to cover costs. If outside the USA, enclose
an international postal reply coupon.

Many of Llewellyn's authors have websites with additional information and resources. For more information, please visit our website at http://www.llewellyn.com.

LOVE

and

INTUITION

A Psychic's Guide
to Creating Lasting Love

SHERRIE DILLARD

Llewellyn Publications
Woodbury, Minnesota

First Edition
First Printing, 2010

Based on a book design by Steffani Sawyer
Cover image © Alan Pappe/Valueline/PunchStock
Cover design by Ellen Dahl
Editing by Brett Fechheimer
Llewellyn is a registered trademark of Llewellyn Worldwide Ltd.

Library of Congress Cataloging-in-Publication Data
Dillard, Sherrie, 1958–
 Love and intuition : a psychic's guide to creating lasting love /
Sherrie Dillard. — 1st ed.
     p. cm.
 ISBN 978-0-7387-1555-1
 1. Love—Miscellanea. 2. Parapsychology. I. Title.
 BF1045.L7D56 2010
 131—dc22
                                    2009052714

Llewellyn Worldwide Ltd. does not participate in, endorse, or have any authority or responsibility concerning private business transactions between our authors and the public.

 All mail addressed to the author is forwarded, but the publisher cannot, unless specifically instructed by the author, give out an address or phone number.

 Any Internet references contained in this work are current at publication time, but the publisher cannot guarantee that a specific location will continue to be maintained. Please refer to the publisher's website for links to authors' websites and other sources.

Llewellyn Publications
Llewellyn Worldwide Ltd.
2143 Wooddale Drive
Woodbury, MN 55125-2989
www.llewellyn.com

Printed in the United States of America

To Amabel Constable and Benjamin Devoid.
Their struggles with love opened a precious door.

Thank you to Carol K. and Carrie Obry.

CONTENTS

INTRODUCTION

~~~~~~

Understanding absolute love is the work of the soul.
The integration of this higher frequency of love
into our everyday life is the work of human evolvement.
The bridge between the two is intuition,
our most powerful and natural wisdom.

[handwritten margin notes: Unconditional love; healthy vs. unhealthy; commitment]

I remember as a child sitting under the big oak trees in my backyard, wiping off my dirty hand and placing it in the steady palm of my best friend. She traced the crooked lines in my palm with the tip of her finger and looked at the little lines that extended from them. She confidently told me that I would marry young and have two children. I knew that she had an aunt who had taught her the basics of palm reading, so I believed her. A jolt of pleasure ran up my spine at the idea of what my future would hold.

Years later, as a young and enthusiastic psychic, after spending a lot of time working with the mysterious beauty of the spiritual world, I found myself answering similar questions for others: Will I meet my soul mate? How can I improve my relationship with my partner? Why do I attract unsatisfying relationships? Does he love me? Is she the right one for me? How can I forgive my ex for all of the lies and betrayal? Will I ever be able to love and trust another person again?

The desire to love and be loved is a consuming inner flame, burning away all other desires and preoccupations. As a psychic reader and intuitive coach, I have responded to these concerns and similar ones for the past twenty-five years. Perhaps more than most other questions that life holds, I've found that people search, with devotion and enthusiasm, the unseen, spiritual realm for guidance in their relationships. My clients include financiers, physicians, scientific researchers, and engineers, as well as writers, artists, and students from all over the world. They are intelligent thinkers and managers of their busy, effective lives, yet they seek, from the unseen and the ethereal, help with their loving relationships.

The Search for Answers

From my palm-reading eight-year-old friend to the business man nervously sitting in my office seeking advice about his love life, my desire to learn more about the way we intuit and the way we love is still strong. When I first began giving professional psychic readings, I did not always know where the answers that I received came from. It was all a mystery to me, too. I would "see" certain people in my mind's eye and describe them to my clients. I would "hear" particular months and days with my inner hearing, and I would receive strong feelings about another's personality traits and their relationship potential.

I did not know how I came to know these things. I just told people whatever information I received. Later, my clients would call or come into my office and tell me that I was right. The person that I described came into their life at the time I said they would, and people would leave relationships when I predicted they would. I became a very busy psychic. But still, I did not understand how I knew—and I wanted to find out.

Learning about Intuition

In my quest to understand my own psychic-intuitive ability, I have learned that intuition is a natural ability that we all share. *Psychic* is just another word for *intuition*. Both words refer to the natural ability we all have to perceive unseen, unknown, subtle frequencies and put words and meaning to these vibrations. For simplicity throughout the book, I use the word *intuitive* rather than *psychic*, but for all intents and purposes, they are essentially the same thing.

Most people become aware of their intuition when it surfaces as spontaneous awareness and an instinctive knowledge of information and knowledge with no rational explanation as to how they know. It is, for example, the sudden, undeniable awareness of another's thoughts or feelings. It is a fluttering in the heart and an unanticipated adrenaline rush that moves through the body when you first meet someone you are attracted to. The remarkable thing about our relationships with other people is that intuitive receptivity is always present. Even people who discount their own intuitive abilities pick up subtle—and sometimes not so subtle—clues about themselves and the important people in their lives. For others, being in a relationship and the closeness it brings dramatically heightens their spiritual sensibilities. After twenty-five years as a practicing psychic, I now know that everyone receives intuitive energy information, and with a little help and practice it can become a reliable source of guidance. Unfortunately, we often ignore or discount the urgings of that inner intuitive voice.

Intuition in Love

My expertise in the intuition-love connection intensified several years ago when I found myself single after many years of marriage. I had been a professional psychic for more than a decade and was confident that I could rely on my abilities to negotiate the ups and downs of attracting and sustaining a soul mate. Was I wrong! Despite my professional experience, accessing intuitive guidance in my own relationships was a bit challenging. I was more accurate with the stranger sitting on my couch than I was in my own concerns. This was not only frustrating; it also didn't make much sense to me. If intuition is a natural ability we all possess, it seems reasonable that everyone, including me, should be able to use it to create happiness and joy in all areas of life.

Making use of intuition in our relationships is difficult because relationships are highly subjective—and emotions, expectations, past patterns, and emotional pain can all get in the way of being able to access useful and accurate guidance.

This interference is a little like the static of a poor phone connection. I was determined to find a way to move through these obstacles and utilize this natural gift in this very important area. I dedicated myself to developing new techniques and trying them out with myself and my clients. In doing so, I discovered that combining basic intuitive development with the energy of absolute love, and learning how to harness the power behind emotions, creates a clear channel for intuitive relationship receptivity. *(emotions fall within 7 chachras)*

Developing deliberate intuition for use in relationships is not simply a matter of information-gathering and observing facts. It goes much deeper than this. Intuition focused in love is the access point to connecting with powerful forces of the soul, where transformation, healing, and deep happiness and joy reside.

Intuitive Love Has No Boundaries

You will find that developing intuitive love provides you with a process for exploring all of your relationship issues and concerns. Throughout this book, we will reveal the answers to many pressing questions: How do I attract my soul mate? How can I restore positive feelings and passion to my current relationship? How can I let go of an unhealthy relationship?

There is no one-size-fits-all answer, but with a thoughtful investigation we will uncover the answers that apply to you.

In addition, opening the door to your innate intuitive ability will grant you many unexpected benefits. Aligning your intuition with the power of love can change your life in mystifying ways. You may, for example, find that you can more quickly navigate and resolve miscommunications and misun-derstandings. You can more easily lift that feeling of grief and despair after the end of a relationship to feel the warm light of hope. You might receive a surprising, conciliatory phone call from an old boyfriend or girlfriend. Feelings of loneliness will subside and your heart will overflow with love. A soul mate may appear after years of failed relationships. You may feel the clear presence of a loved one who has passed over. You will experience an overwhelming inner assurance that there is a wise and loving force guiding your path. Guilt and anger are replaced with forgiveness and compassion. Experiencing increased intimacy and the kind of deep connection that you've always desired with your partner, you will become a force of healing for others. Intuition focused in love makes us whole and nourishes our lives in a multitude of ways.

The Process

In my first book, *Discover Your Psychic Type: Developing and Using Your Natural Intuition*, I outline one of the most important dis-coveries I've made in my career as a psychic. Just as every per-son has unique talents and traits, intuition surfaces uniquely in our individual lives as well. I have found that intuition naturally surfaces in our lives largely in four different ways—and *Discover Your Psychic Type* offers many ideas for how to understand and develop these unique skills. It has proved to be a highly effective way to develop intuition and to understand oneself.

In this book, I take the four intuitive types into the arena of love and relationships. You will discover your innate intui-tive type in love, and the unique relationship characteristics of each type. Not only does your intuitive type give you information about yourself and the world around you—it also offers insight into the way you love, the way those who you are in relationship with love you, and your relationship strengths and weaknesses.

Section I begins with a quiz to determine your unique intuitive-love type. You will discover how your intuitive-love type influences your choices, decisions, and behavior in the realm of love and relationships. This section provides a foundational nine-step process that will allow you to develop intuition specifically in the area of love and relationships.

Section II shows you how to successfully use the intuition-love connection in your relationships. Relationships are lessons in love. They steer you to the places within yourself where you most need to heal, grow, and experience joy. I'll offer new, deeper ways of looking at relationships and how you can better attract the right partner, relate to your partner, and create a long, lasting relationship. True healing is the full recognition and expression of your most loving self. It is the transformative journey from relative love to fully integrated absolute love in your innermost being, in your relationships, and in your life. The need for healing is not only from physical pain or trauma. It can be from the subtle suffering that is a by-product of living in our world. You cannot help but be affected by the fears, negative beliefs, and judgments of everyday life. You were born into a world that is still learning what love is. Healing is living your full potential without limitation. This section explores this kind of healing.

In section III, we look at how the intuition-love connection can infuse you with sensual vibrancy and magnetism. There are many facets of intuition that can open you to new worlds and new experiences. Using a step-by-step intuitive approach, this section shows you how to use your intuition to attract a soul mate, increase intimacy, and heighten sensuality. Developing your intuitive-love type energetically draws to you the kind of relationships that truly satisfy.

The universe is overflowing with love, which is ours for the taking. In section IV, you will learn how to become aware of the love and guidance that is always available to you. With deliberate intuition, you will increase your ability to communicate and participate with your angels and spirit guides and loved ones in spirit. Aligning yourself with your powerful spiritual allies allows for the entrance of a remarkable love.

How to Use This Book

Note: The names and identifying details of the people mentioned in this book have been changed, in order to protect their confidentiality.

You cannot learn about love or intuition simply by reading about it. You must experience it. For this reason, I have included easy-to-follow exercises and meditations for all levels of intuitive ability. Everyone from the novice intuitive to the adept psychic will find themselves empowered and encouraged to take their unique intuitive potential to the next level of proficiency. Even if you lack confidence in your intuitive abilities, you will soon discover the innate intuitive potential within you.

Take your time with each chapter. Practice the exercises. You do not have to master each step before moving to the next. Some skills or understanding may come quickly and others may not.

In my many years of being a professional psychic and counselor, I have known some lonely single and unhappily married people. I have also witnessed clients and friends using the intuition-love connection to attract loving partners, inject passion into their current relationships, and become lovingly content within themselves.

Whether your desire is to attract a soul mate, heal and revitalize your current relationship, explore the intuition-love connection, or understand love and relationships through the eyes of a psychic, I hope these pages will enlighten and inspire you.

PART I

Nine Steps to Intuitive-Love Mastery

1

STEP 1: ACCEPT YOUR
NATURAL INTUITION

～～～～～～～～～～～～～～～～～～～～～～～～～～～～～～～

Feelings of love and connection have accompanied my intuitive awareness as far back as I can remember. Even when the source of who or what loved me was hidden and unknown, I felt comfort and warmth in my communication with that source. Not everyone feels this way. For many people, sixth-sensory events and their own intuition feel odd and abstract. The thought that we are invisibly connected to one another is a difficult leap. Yet, we are always in relationship.

We define our world, and the world defines us; there is a constant interplay. The stars, interspersed in the night sky, eventually give way to the dawn. The dawn brings forth the day, which ultimately relinquishes its light to the darkness. We are held safely in this consistent rhythm, and we live, unknowingly, in relationship and connection with all living beings. Though we appear to be scattered, separate, and often opposed, our longing for love and connection draws us back to the truth of our oneness. It is through the desire to love and be loved that

13

we are able to break down our sense of aloneness and become aware of our interconnectedness.

Love Strengthens Intuition

Your connection with all of life is often expressed through spontaneous intuitive awareness. Although at times it is quiet and barely noticeable, your intuition is always present and attempting to guide you in the direction of relationship bliss and fulfillment. We often repress and ignore the unwavering inner intuitive voice, only to later realize its accuracy and trustworthiness.

You might, for instance, deny that subtle but persistent feeling that, despite your attraction to a certain person, the relationship could be troublesome. Or, you might ignore the sense that you *know* how to heal a broken relationship. Intuition often surfaces through surprising feelings or an ache or a quivering heart. Have you ever had a strong sense of knowing someone you've only just met or experienced a confusing pang in the stomach? These are intuitive cues; listen to them. Even when there is no apparent reason for your attraction to another person, you may discover later that this person provides you with unexpected benefits and advantages and brings a new positive perspective into your life.

Sometimes an intuitive jolt strikes and we pay attention. This happened to me years ago after having driven the long journey from New England to northern California to relocate. On the day that I arrived, tired and weary, I noticed a young man walking out the front door of the house adjacent to the one where I would be staying. In a flash of surprise, I said to myself, "Oh, that's what he looks like." I had an instantaneous and unshakable inner knowing that this stranger would be an important person in my life. And I was right. I ended up marrying him.

Activating Your Intuition

Love itself seems to activate intuition. Intuition is the deep and wordless sharing between two souls, and it is not coincidental that your intuition seems stronger when beginning a relationship. Intimacy and feelings of love and affection between people intensify intuitive and unspoken communication. Even if you do not consciously recognize the strong, intuitive connection with another, you are still picking up constant and spontaneous clues. You may, for instance, experience unexpected feelings of sadness, joy, anxiety, or stress—and wonder where those emotions are coming from. You assume they are your own feelings, but they may not be. Have you ever had a sudden awareness or perception about a loved one who isn't present? Maybe you rationalize it as daydreaming or fantasy when, in fact, your loved one is actually communicating with you through thoughts and feelings.

Answers in Action

Intuition not only sends us messages; it can also lead us into what appears to be a random circumstance or situation, where we discover answers to our questions or concerns. This may be a chance encounter or a seemingly frustrating event. Often when we have exhausted all options, something, which goes counter to our logical approach, unexpectedly surfaces.

Darien

Darien first came to see me at the prompting of his sister. Although he was initially shy, toward the end of the session he excitedly shared the story of how he had met his new wife. He told me that he had searched long and hard for the woman of his dreams. He went to singles events and was an active member of an Internet dating site, and although he'd met many women, none touched his heart.

On his way to work one day he was stopped at a light. Without warning, a compact car plowed into the back of his new sedan, jerking him backward. He pulled over to the side of the street, head throbbing and annoyed that he was now going to be late for an important meeting. His annoyance grew to frustration as he saw the compact pull into a parking lot a block ahead. Darien got back into his car and pulled into the parking lot, got out, and tapped on the offender's window. A small woman with dark hair opened the door and got out. He looked into her eyes and almost forgot about the damage to his new car. He told me that he knew, with more conviction than he had ever felt about anything else, that this was no accident. In those few seconds he felt as if this could be the woman he had been searching for.

The Various Ways Intuition Surfaces

Many sudden, intuitive connections happen through telepathy, which is the ability to tune in to and know the thoughts of another. Telepathic communication can happen unintentionally or deliberately between two people or within groups of people who have learned the skill of sending and receiving messages. Quite often, telepathy and clairaudience, the ability to receive intuitive information through inner hearing, will emerge together.

Anthony

Anthony, a heavy-equipment operator, had always believed in his intuition. His belief was confirmed recently through an unexpected intuitive occurrence he had on his way to work one busy morning. As he drove down a familiar stretch of highway, his mind wandered to thoughts of his wife, whom he had left sleeping not too long ago. As hard as Anthony tried to shake it, he had a sense of excited anticipation about her. He kept hearing her voice, asking him to come home. The message was so persistent that he decided to turn his truck around and head back home. When he arrived he hurried into the house, calling his wife's name. He heard her faint reply coming from the bathroom. He quickly opened the door and found her with tears in her eyes, standing next to the sink and holding a slim white piece of plastic. She looked lovingly into his eyes as she told him that the test was positive. After months of trying, she was pregnant.

Intuitive Seeing and Bodily Sensations

Intuitive connections can often be felt in the body. The experience of spontaneous intuitive sensations throughout the body is referred to as *clairsentience*. This might be felt as a gut feeling, a hunch, a stirring in the heart, or a tingling on the skin or head. This often happens when you first meet someone. It might be that your inner knowing is sending a message of compatibility and connection with another, or it could be a warning to be alert.

Claire

My friend Claire loves to tell the story of how she met Kent, her husband of many years. Soon after she graduated from college, Claire began to pursue a career in law. She had always wanted to work in the district attorney's office as a lawyer, and she approached her career with devotion and the necessary hard work. Before work one early morning, she went to the gym to join in a cycling class. She felt her heart skip a beat when a man took the bike beside hers. He was average looking, not her type, and she was not looking to date. She was working out hard and thus interpreted the leap in her heart as exercise overexertion. A few days later she was back in the gym, in the same class with the same man seated near her. This time she felt butterflies in her stomach, and when he met her at the water cooler after class, she felt a shiver move up her spine.

At first she was curious as to why she would feel these physical sensations, as she had no attraction to this man and was not interested in dating. However, over the next several weeks, the same scenario occurred over and over: he would sit near her and they would talk after class. She discovered in their conversations that they had similar interests and that he too was an attorney. One morning he nervously asked her to go hiking the following weekend, and she accepted. They had a great time and set up another date for later in the week. Again they had a wonderful time, and even though she was still not "ready" to date, her body told her a different story. After dinner when he came close to saying goodbye, she felt another surge of energy move up her spine. She passionately met his kiss—and, as she tells the story, "the rest is history."

Intuitive Feeling

While some people like Claire receive intuitive energy in their body, others unconsciously soak in the emotions and feelings of others. This is referred to as *empathy*, and it may be the most common form of spontaneous intuitive awareness that occurs in relationships. Empathy is the ability to receive and tune in to the emotional state of a person or a group. Quite often people are not aware of their intuitive capacity to feel the emotions of others. Because this happens so often and so naturally, it is easy to mistake these intuited feelings as one's own and become confused and overwhelmed by them. Empathy is so common between people that we are often not consciously aware of it, or it doesn't seem unusual. Empathy can encourage communication and intimacy between people. When we feel what others feel, we are more likely to be understanding and compassionate toward them. However, being overly empathetic can cause us to miss important intuitive information. Finding the right balance between tuning in to the emotional energy in a relationship and being able to be objective and clear can take some practice.

Jalen

Jalen had a nagging, intuitive sense that her partner Zach was interested in another woman. She had felt his feelings toward her change a month or two earlier, and with each day that passed he seemed to become more emotionally distant. When

Jalen shared her intuitive sense with Zach, he told her she was being silly. He claimed to be very much in love with her and was not, he told her, interested in anyone else. Because he seemed so taken aback by her suggestion that there might be someone else, and because she felt that she would hurt his feelings by questioning him, Jalen began to distrust her intuitive impressions. So, she ignored them. A few weeks later, Zach said he was leaving Jalen for someone else, a woman he had been secretly dating for months.

Trusting her intuition may not have saved her feelings of hurt or kept her relationship intact, but it might have helped her to tune in to guidance that could support and guide her in this difficult time.

Spiritual Receptivity

We also intuitively receive guidance, help, and support from the nonphysical realms. This happens quite naturally in everyday life. Without your knowing it, the source of some of your seemingly random ideas, insights, and chance encounters come from the loving direction of angels, guides, and loved ones in spirit. While you experience yourself as a physical being, they know you as spirit and soul. They connect to you through dreams, prayer, meditation, the natural world, and synchronistic events in your everyday life. Despite the physical boundaries that seem to separate us, we are in constant communication with all of life.

Defying Logic

As you increase your intuitive receptiveness, you may find that intuition steers you in a direction that may be surprising or may conflict with your ego's agenda and desires. The ego is that part of us that feels separate from the greater whole. The ego often perceives love as distant and unattainable. Intuition instead is always firmly rooted in the interconnectedness of all of life. It is not controlled by preconceived limitations, judgments, and conditions, and it can bypass what you believe is possible. When you listen to and act on your intuitive knowing, you may be surprised and mystified by what happens in your relationships.

Chase

I first met Chase when he came to see me at the urging of his wife, Fiona, who had recently met me for a reading. They met in the Midwest, when Chase was there visiting his brother. His sister-in-law and Fiona were best friends, and when Chase literally bumped into her at a small family gathering, sparks flew. They decided to try to maintain a relationship, but because of his hectic work schedule, Fiona was the one traveling from the Midwest to the East Coast, where Chase lived. When Chase asked Fiona to marry him one year after their initial meeting, she quit her job and moved into his home.

A year or so later, Fiona's family decided to take a trip together to Europe. Since her marriage, Fiona didn't see her family as much, so she was excited about the upcoming trip. Chase thought about the proposed trip for a few days and told Fiona that while it was a great idea, it was not a good time for him to leave work. Fiona was upset. She did not under-stand why this trip was not important to him. Chase became frustrated by what he felt was Fiona's insistence that he go to Europe with her. She would have her family, and there would be plenty to do. He became annoyed and then angry that Fiona did not seem to understand his demanding work schedule. The more he thought about it, the more upset he became.

While driving to work a few days later, Chase unexpect-edly felt his deceased father's spirit there with him in the car. This was a new sensation for Chase; since his father's death more than five years previously, he had not felt his presence as real and tangibly as he did then. He felt his father's warm and friendly demeanor, assuring him that he was fine. He remem-bered his father's quiet and stable personality. Chase could always depend on his father to do what he said he would do. He was a trustworthy man of few words.

As his father's presence began to diminish, Chase's thoughts and feelings turned to Fiona. He wanted her to understand him and support his needs. Chase couldn't under-stand why his wife was being so demanding. As he reviewed his last conversation with her, he felt an unexpected quiet pres-ence emerge within him. His mind went blank for a moment and again he felt his father's strong presence, this time urging him to go to Europe. The firmness of this message surprised him, in part because it was so different from what he wanted to do. He did not like flying or crowded places. He could think of so many reasons not to go, but he could not shake his father's message. Fiona was thrilled when Chase went home that evening and let her know that he wanted to be a part of the upcoming family European adventure.

Six months after their trip, Fiona's mother died unexpectedly. Now, each night before going to sleep, Chase looks with comfort at the framed photo of him with Fiona and her parents in front of the Eiffel Tower. In it, Fiona has one arm around Chase and the other around her mother; she looks as happy as he has ever seen her. His decision, prompted by his intuition, was the right one.

Life-Changing Intuitive Realizations

A sudden intuitive insight can create lasting changes in our lives. Intuition operates outside of the parameters of time, distance, and condition. We may struggle with an issue for some time—then seemingly out of nowhere a sudden realization provides the needed awareness.

Bother parity

Jeff

Jeff has always been thought of by most of our mutual friends as a handsome and dynamic man who has trouble committing to a relationship. He has no problem attracting and dating women, but his relationships never last long. Even though he claims to want a committed, long-term relationship and possibly marriage, Jeff just never seemed to be able to find the right person. He flitted from one woman to another, never satisfied or happy. Jeff said that he was confused by his own behavior. He thought he must have some issues with commitment but couldn't figure out how to change.

One morning while in the shower after a rigorous game of racquetball, he had a sudden and profound flash of insight that his purpose in life was to learn how to commit his love and devote himself to another. Jeff realized that he was looking for the right person to satisfy him, and it was now clear to him that he, instead, was meant to give of himself and to love another unselfishly. The insight seemed simple, yet it struck a deep chord within him. He knew, without a doubt, that this was the truth.

A change of behavior after this event was not difficult. Instead of trying to impress and charm women, he began to share of himself at a deeper level and listen to others as they spoke. Within a year he met Jamie, a friend of a co-worker. She was gentle and kind. He felt his heart open when he met her, and he felt a warmth in her presence that he never wanted to be without.

Exercise

Intuition is so intertwined within our relationships that we seldom recognize it. Yet we all have an invisible support system that is always observing, guiding, and steering us toward our highest good, even when we are not conscious of it. As you become more conscious of your intuition, you will find that it has a purposeful and important task in your life.

Journaling

Your first step in developing deliberate intuition for use in relationships is to become aware of your ever-present and innate intuition. Keeping an *intuition journal* is a good way to become aware of when your intuition is at work, as well as providing you with insight into your intuitive strengths, weaknesses, and overall intuitive-development progress. Throughout this book I provide exercises, meditations, and visualizations that require you to write down your observations and experiences. In your journal, you can also record hunches, gut feelings, synchronicities, dreams, spontaneous thoughts or sensations, and feelings that occur. Even if they seem to make no sense or feel inconsequential or frivolous, record them anyway.

You can begin your intuition journal by writing about those times in your life when your intuition spontaneously surfaced. Sometimes it is not until later that we are able to see and understand an experience as intuitive. Often what appears to be a mistake, a lucky break, or a missed opportunity is really the presence of a deep, inner knowing that is directing your path. Reflect upon the times that your intuition guided you. This simple act will begin the bridge between your conscious awareness and your often-hidden intuition.

2

STEP 2: DISCOVER YOUR INTUITIVE-LOVE TYPE

~~~~~~~~~~~~~~~~~~~~~~~~~~~~~~~~~~

As you pay more attention to spontaneous episodes of intuitive awareness, you will soon discover that your intuition is as unique as you are. The second step to developing intuitive love is to discover your innate intuitive type in love and relationships.

Even when you are not aware of it, your intuition is silently absorbing invisible energy information through your thoughts, your emotions, your body, or your energy field. Have you ever felt a wave of emotion come over you, and you wonder if these feelings may be coming from your partner—or you suddenly know the thoughts of another, without knowing how you know? Have you ever felt anxious, tense, or stressed for no discernible reason and later found out that at that same time your partner was undergoing a stressful and anxiety-producing event? Maybe you have had dreams of meeting a soul mate and then met a person who bears an uncanny resemblance to the person in your dream?

These are just some of the ways that we regularly pick up intuitive information. Intuitive receptivity is so common in relationships that you may not even notice it. As you become more familiar with the particular way that you naturally receive intuitive information, you will be better able to harness these and other spontaneous and seemingly random intuitive episodes into reliable relationship guidance.

Your Intuitive Type

The four basic intuitive types are mental, emotional, spiritual, and physical. Each one describes an innate way that people naturally absorb and receive intuitive energy. Love is powerful energy and your intuitive-love type will provide you with insight into how you love and how others love you.

Understanding your natural intuitive predisposition will empower you to develop deliberate intuition with more ease and confidence. It will also give you important insight into how you intuit and express love.

To determine your intuitive-love type, answer the following questions, and then tally your results based on the instructions at the end of the quiz. You will most likely feel all possible answers are true, so circle the one that seems to be your *strongest* tendency. There is a more extensive quiz in my first book, *Discover Your Psychic Type*. You can use the two quizzes together to fine-tune your intuition to new and exciting levels.

1. I am most comfortable with others who:
    a. discuss their ideas
    b. share their feelings
    c. participate in activities
    (d.) seek spiritual growth

2. When a relationship ends I am most likely to:
    (a.) try and figure out what happened and why
    b. grieve and seek out supportive friends and family
    c. get busy, with work or recreational activities
    d. meditate on the lessons and purpose of the
        relationship

3. I express love most often by:
    a. understanding others
    b. feeling what others feel
    c. acts of service
    (d.) offering inspiration and positive energy

4. When I sense that my partner is detaching from the
    relationship, I:
    a. share my impressions and try to discuss what I sense is
        happening
    b. tell my partner that I love him (or her) and try to elicit
        his (or her) love in various ways
    (c.) become more sensual and sexual
    d. say nothing, meditate, and look to my dreams for guid-
        ance

5. I am most likely to seek the help of angels and spirit guides when:
    a. I need a solution to a problem
    b. I need to feel loved
    c. I am more comfortable with fairies and nature spirits
    d. I want companionship

6. I know a relationship is over when:
    a. we no longer share the same ideas and goals, or see things the same way
    b. I am no longer in love
    c. I am no longer physically attracted
    d. I have learned what I needed to learn in the relationship

7. Without knowing how, I often have insight into others':
    a. thoughts
    b. emotions
    c. physical health
    d. dreams and aspirations

8. My perfect date would include:
    a. a long, interesting discussion under a moonlit night sky
    b. feeling my heart open with the warm glow of passion
    c. being close, holding hands, cuddling, or warm hugs
    d. being in the presence of a kindred spirit, with electrifying feelings of soul connection

9. Without being told, I can tune in to what is going on in a relationship by:
   a. intuiting my partner's thoughts
   b. feeling the emotional energy that I receive from him or her
   c. the sensations and feelings in my body, primarily my gut feelings and overall feelings of tension or stress
   d. I just know, not sure how, that I need to trust my impressions and inner knowing

10. When I am not in an intimate relationship, what I miss most is:
   a. the synergy of common thoughts, ideas, and mutual understanding
   b. an open and expanded love-filled heart, sharing deep feelings
   c. being close, and relaxing in shared activities and sensual and sexual pleasure
   d. not fulfilling my soul's purpose of deeply loving and evolving with another

11. I become restless in intimate relationships when:
   a. I am not mentally challenged
   b. the emotional intensity fades
   c. when physical intimacy no longer excites me
   d. when I sense I have fulfilled my purpose in it

12. I feel instant chemistry with others who:
   a. expand my mind and stimulate new ideas
   b. open my heart
   c. send tingling sensations and shivers through my body
   d. inspire me

13. When I am not feeling loved, I:
    (a.) try to figure out why
    b. feel all kinds of feelings, like sadness, loneliness, or frustration, or hope and optimism
    c. feel stressed and physically tired
    d. feel disconnected and spacey

14. When I am in love, I can easily tune in to my partner's:
    a. thoughts
    b. feelings
    c. health and well-being
    (d.) spiritual energy

15. When my loved ones are experiencing difficulties, I:
    a. listen and offer insightful ideas and suggestions
    b. feel what they feel and encourage them to express their feelings
    c. hold their hand, cook meals, run errands for them
    (d.) pray for them, send healing energy, discern the deeper message

16. I am aware of the presence of loved ones who have passed over when:
    (a.) I am given a new idea or helpful insight
    b. I feel comforted and watched over
    c. I smell a certain perfume or cigar scent or my body tingles with warmth
    d. I see them

17. It is most important that a mate:
    a. accepts me
    (b.) passionately shares with me

c. helps me

d. is on a similar spiritual path

18. I would like to believe that all of life is in a wonderful conspiracy to:

a. teach me how to fully love another

b. satisfy my desire for a soul-mate relationship

c. help me to create the best life and relationships that are
possible

d. reveal to me my purpose in love

19. One of my secret wishes is to:

a. tune in to and know others' thoughts and foresee the
future

b. heal others with the power of my love

c. transmit healing to others through my touch

d. be a medium and psychic, and give messages of love and
support to others from the spirit world

20. I feel closest to others when:

a. we share our thoughts

b. we share our feelings

c. we participate in a mutually satisfying activity together

d. we have the same spiritual ideals

21. The highest form of love is best expressed as:

a. enlightenment

b. heartfelt compassion, forgiveness, and unconditional love

c. feelings of oneness and unity with all of life

d. sensations of soothing energy, lifting one beyond the
mundane and into bliss

22. In the ultimate love relationship:
    a. the truth of love and life will be revealed to me
    b. my heart will expand and dissolve into a greater love
    c. I will experience oneness and complete union with another
    d. I will break through the limitations of the physical realm and achieve mystical transcendence

Tally up your results. If your predominant letter is:
    a. you are a mental intuitive   8
    b. you are an emotional intuitive 3
    c. you are a physical intuitive   2
    d. you are a spiritual intuitive   9

Most people are a combination of the different types. Be aware of your predominant intuitive-love type and also the type or types that you are least aligned with.

Exercise

The following is a stream-of-consciousness exercise that will help you to further explore your intuitive type. Using this technique, you simply write for a period of time without stopping, monitoring, or censoring what you are writing. It is the writing that invites the inner intuitive voice to emerge. Even if you do not know what to write or if you write nonsense, just go with it. Eventually a deeper part of you will begin to surface.

Stream of Consciousness

Think of a person with whom you are or were in a past or present relationship. Now, for five minutes, without stopping or lifting your pen or pencil from the paper, write about that person. Write whatever comes to you; do not censor or edit anything. There is no right or wrong. You cannot make a mistake.

When you finish, close your eyes and allow an image of the person to form in your mind's eye. Observe the image and allow any information, thoughts, impressions, sensations, or feelings to surface. Stay in this quiet receptive state for several minutes. Then, open your eyes and write another paragraph about that person.

Finally, read what you have just written. What impressions did you receive? How did you describe him or her? Was it more a physical, emotional, spiritual, or mental description? What is your relationship with the person? Do you have a strong emotional connection with him or her?

Intuitive-Type Responses

An *emotional* intuitive naturally absorbs the emotions and feelings of others. Emotional intuitives are naturally empathetic; they tend to feel what others feel and make loving and devoted partners.

Emotional intuitives typically write about a person who elicits strong feelings and will often describe a person by their emotional characteristics.

Karen wrote about a man that she has been dating for just a few months. She described how on their first awkward date she felt an uncanny warmth and kindness while sitting and drinking coffee with him. Just looking in his eyes, she wrote, she felt a tender caring that opened her heart.

A *mental* intuitive telepathically intuits others' thoughts and ideas and is attuned to systems and patterns. With their keen intuitive awareness, they easily understand others, intuit solutions to problems and difficulties, and are able to perceive future outcomes.

They will describe the person's intelligence, describe common ideas, or list facts about him or her.

Jeff wrote about his girlfriend, Lana. He described her recent promotion at work, their common personal and career goals, and their shared ideas on most topics.

A *physical* intuitive soaks in the energy of others and the environment primarily through his or her body. He or she can also receive information by holding objects, looking at pictures, and holding hands or touching another. They absorb energy information into their body, and because of this often discount their intuitive ability.

A physical intuitive will describe a person's physical characteristics and, perhaps, recall a memory of an event that they shared together.

Roy described his wife, Clarice, as attractive and fun to be with. They both enjoy the water, and he wrote at length about a recent vacation they spent snorkeling in Costa Rica.

A *spiritual* intuitive intuits by attuning himself or herself to energy. These intuitives may receive information through precognitive dreams, visions, and the spontaneous awareness of angels and loved ones in spirit. They can be interesting, sensitive partners who are often misunderstood.

A spiritual intuitive describes a person in more ethereal terms. He or she may tune in to the person's energy and even uncover new information. Julie wrote about her partner, Eddy. She wrote about his inner depth and the soulful connection they shared. She expressed that their connection bypasses words.

You will most likely describe your person in all of these different ways. Look for a salient tendency and consider your initial observations. Most people show some characteristics of each of the four types, yet will notice one particular intuitive strength.

Different Paths, Same Destination

Although each psychic type receives intuitive energy in a different way, the information received may be the same. Take, for example, the story of Mona and Duane. Mona wanted to attract a loving partner, and decided to enlist her intuition to help her. Unbeknownst to her, a soul mate is on the same journey; his name is Duane. Mona and Duane have mutual friends, Lisa and Ray.

Lisa and Ray plan to celebrate the purchase of their new home by inviting a few friends in for a party. Lisa, a spiritual intuitive, is Mona's close friend. She would like to help Mona meet a loving partner. Lisa had a dream about Mona a week before the housewarming party. In the dream, Mona was in a beautiful cathedral wearing a long, white wedding gown. She was standing beside an altar of flowers and candles; next to her stood the dark-haired groom. Lisa's husband, Ray, stood next to the man. Ray had his arm around the mystery groom, and was smiling and singing. Lisa recorded the dream in her journal and intuits that Ray may have something to do with Mona's meeting her future husband.

The next morning Lisa asked Ray to invite some of his friends to the party. Ray adds some golfing buddies to the list. At work that day, he passes Duane's desk. Duane had transferred to the area recently and had been with the company for just a few weeks. Ray stops to ask him some questions about his accounts and picks up an interesting antique pencil holder sitting on the desk. Ray is a physical intuitive, and when he picks up the pencil holder he instantly feels a warm, positive connection to Duane. He knows that they will be friends, and later that evening he asks Lisa to send an invitation to him.

Mona is an emotional intuitive, and when she receives her party invitation, she feels her heart leap for joy. She can't explain why, but she is happy all day.

Across town, Duane receives his invitation to the house warming, which he notices will be held on a Sunday, May 22, at 2:00 pm. He quickly realizes that he has been glancing at the clock every afternoon at 2:00 and has even begun to wake at 2:00 in the morning. Interesting, he thinks, May 22 was his father's birthday, and his father died two years ago. Could it simply be a coincidence that the number 2 keeps popping up in his life? Not likely, he thinks, and quickly accepts the invitation. He knows it is important for him to attend. Duane is a mental intuitive.

The day of the party, Mona arrives early to help Lisa with some last-minute preparations. She is feeling unusually positive and optimistic. Duane also heads to the party early, thinking that perhaps he can also lend a hand. When Duane enters the house he immediately locks eyes, in what feels like an eternal moment, with Mona, who is filling glass trays with mints and strawberries.

Although intuition surfaced in a different way for each person, there was a wonderful conspiracy of intuitive events that brought these two destined soul mates, Duane and Mona, together.

As you become more sensitive as to how your intuition surfaces, you will not only be able to fully develop your intuitive potential, you will also discover that it provides you with a unique way to understand yourself and others.

Seven Intuitive Skills

Now that you are more familiar with the way that you receive intuitive energy information, you can further develop it. In the same way you learn to speak a foreign language or play a musical instrument—with instruction, practice, and dedication—you can learn how to direct the spontaneous episodes of intuitive insight into effective and reliable intuitive ability. With a little motivation and enthusiasm, you can harness your innate intuitive type and use it at will. Don't be fooled into believing that intuitive abilities are rare gifts. This will only serve to block your inherent intuitive awareness, which is as natural to us as love itself.

Following is a set of seven skills for you to use through-out the book. These skills can help you gain confidence and strengthen your intuitive muscle.

1. Observe
Observe and listen. Pay attention to your inner voice, any physical sensations, persistent yet subtle thoughts, feelings, images, flashes of color or light, gut feelings, or any other sensations that might occur. Do not expect your intuition to surface in any particular way. Simply observe without judgment.

Try this. Close your eyes, and take a few deep breaths. Then, repeat this several times: "I am love." Rest and observe. In your journal, record whatever feelings, sensations, impressions, and images that surface. Go behind your conscious thoughts, and observe the subtleties that emerge.

2. Imagine
Imagination is your intuition's best friend. Imagination is the faculty that your consciousness uses to put meaning to the energy it experiences. Most people feel like they are just making things up. If you feel that way, great! Keep it up.

Try this. Imagine yourself doing something that inspires you to be deliriously happy. What's happening? Write it down in your journal, with abandon. Do not judge. Do not censor. Simply write it all down.

3. Take a Leap
You will never be sure if your intuition is accurate until you take a leap. The logical mind always wants to have control of

any situation. Don't let it. Go with what comes to you no matter how outrageous or obvious it may seem. Jump!

Try this. Think of a loved one who has died. Imagine that
person sitting across from you. He or she has a message for
you. Repeat it out loud. Leap into the unknown and imagine
what his or her thoughts are. Don't worry about the outcome.
Just enjoy the process.

4. Make Mistakes

It is as important to be wrong as it is to be right when developing your intuition. As you learn to recognize the subtle sensations and feelings of your intuition at work, you will be able to
differentiate between your intuition and your mind chatter.

Intuitive information can often be felt in the body as an
uplifting and stimulating buzz, or a feeling of lightness and con-
centrated persistent energy. My friend Sara knows her psychic
perception is at work when she gets what she calls goose bumps,
tingling sensations up and down her arms. But you won't develop
this sensitivity until you've gotten it wrong a few times.

Try this. Hold a piece of unopened mail, or focus on an
unopened e-mail from a friend or loved one. Close your eyes
and imagine any words, numbers, and other information that it
contains. Check in with your body: how does it feel, what are
these sensations telling you about the contents of the mail or
e-mail? Write down in your journal whatever comes to you.

5. Receive

Develop the habit of accepting whatever you receive. Imagine
that you are an open channel for wise and loving guidance. Don't

waste a moment trying to figure everything out in advance. Relax and be receptive and open to any and all intuitive guidance. Be receptive to any body sensations, thoughts, emotions, dreams, visions, images, and flashes of knowing—and accept, without judgment, your experience.

Try this. In your journal, write down all of your responses to the following: "My biggest step in love is . . ."

Don't overthink it. Just let the answers flow.

6. Interpret

Do not jump to conclusions or try to make sense of the intuitive impressions that you receive. Become comfortable with not knowing. Stop yourself from overanalyzing the process or the information. To interpret accurately your intuitive information, you must: listen, have patience, and allow it to evolve in its own way. Repeat the exercises in this set. Intense focusing or analyzing only stifles intuitive growth. Like fine wine, interpreting your intuitive information takes time to come to maturity.

Try this. Use your imagination and create an image or symbol that represents love. Draw it. Keep it in mind as you read this book and in your relationships to better understand what this symbol means to you.

7. Have fun

Don't be afraid to laugh at yourself and all the wonderful and wild impressions, accurate insights, and mistakes that you receive. Have a good time learning about yourself and love. Do not take yourself or this process too seriously. The more you laugh, the more love you receive.

Try this. In your journal, write down the silliest thing that you have ever done when you were in love.

Leave and Come Back

Record your impressions. Interpret them as best you can. Then let them go. Quite often, the information and guidance we receive does not make sense at first. Close your journal and put it away. When you come back to it later, you will be surprised how much clarity this separation has provided.

3

STEP 3: THE BASICS:
RECEIVE—IMAGINE—INTERPRET

People are often surprised when I tell them that developing deliberate intuition is not a mystical and supernatural phenomenon. It is instead a process that is relatively straightforward and uncomplicated. The third step in developing intuitive love is to learn the basic intuitive building blocks. They are the ability to consciously receive energy, translate this energy into impressions, and interpret the impressions into usable information.

Consciously Receive Energy

Each intuitive type—emotional, mental, physical, and spiritual—receives intuitive energy in a particular way. Spending time in quiet reflection and inner listening will help you better tune in to the way that you receive intuitive energy. It may be difficult at first to differentiate intuitive impulses from normal, conscious inner ramblings. When you are in a quiet, meditative state, look for these telltale signs of intuitive receptivity.

Emotional. A common intuitive signal for the emotional intuitive is the random and inexplicable surfacing of feelings and emotions. Intuitive emotions can feel either intense or faint. There is a subtle difference between individual emotions and emotions that are being intuitively absorbed from the environment. If you are not sure of the source of what you are feeling, simply draw your attention inward and quietly ask whether what you are feeling are your own emotions. The answer will surface with surprising ease.

Mental. A mental intuitive receives information through a direct knowing, which differs from linear thinking. Intuitive direct knowing feels like information is being dropped on you out of nowhere. It is not an analytical chain of thought or mind chatter. It is information that comes without rational thought, and it often contradicts our logical mind.

Physical. A physical intuitive is likely to receive intuitive impulses through bodily sensations, especially those in the stomach and solar plexus. These sensations may be accompanied with a sense of knowing, confidence, feelings of increased physical energy, or feelings of apathy and depletion. These intuitives need to pay attention and tune in to their normal physical energy levels and how the body feels. This will help them discern when they are receiving intuitive energy and when the physical sensations are their own.

Spiritual. A spiritual intuitive receives intuitive energy through tingling sensations or feelings of expansion and heightened vibration that seems to surround him or her. Intuition may surface through the visual perception of colors–pink, white, purple, gold, red, or yellow. These intuitives may also more readily sense the presence of angels or loved ones in spirit. Many spiritual intuitives receive intuitive information through dreams, visions, and premonitions.

Translating Energy

The next step in harnessing the power of your intuitive type is to translate energy into impressions. Your intuitive receptivity is an aspect of your multidimensional nature that, regardless of how you try, cannot be fully ignored or silenced. We are all equipped with a masterful and intricate inner energetic processor that can decipher and convert nonsensical energy into understandable information. Mastering your inner intuitive potential is not as difficult as it may appear. The simple and often misunderstood gift of imagination is the key to unlocking your intuitive potential.

The Question

There is an essential question to ask, and it will guide you through the process of interpreting intuitive energy. It can make the difference between your being overwhelmed and confused by intuitive energy or your becoming a highly skilled intuitive. The question is: "If this energy I am receiving were an image, what would it be?" It doesn't matter if the energy presents as emotional waves, spontaneous knowing, tingling, physical sensations of expansion, tightness, or waves of subtle energy. What is the image?

Next, close your eyes and allow an image—literal or figurative, a symbol, number, name, letter, or word—to emerge.

This is where your imagination and your ability to pretend come in. Don't try to sort it out mentally, just ask your own inner knowing to translate the energy into images. Expect it to feel as though you are using your imagination and that you are just making it up. You are. Imagination is the powerful tool that we all possess that translates higher-level energy into a form we can understand.

Practice Moving Energy to Image

Try this exercise to help you transform the energy you receive into an image. When you finish each one, record the experience and information in your journal.

To begin, sit quietly and comfortably. Relax and close your eyes. Then, imagine a symbol for each of the following:

Vulnerability

Joy

Forgiveness

Anxiety

Again, close your eyes and now imagine that each of these is a color. What color would each be?

Compassion

Affection

Fear

Lust

Now, close your eyes and feel the texture of the following sensations:

Pleasure

Disappointment

Ecstasy

Sadness

Finally, close your eyes and imagine that the following each have a place somewhere in your body. Where would they be?

Kindness

Longing

Peace

Serenity

Stress

Move into an observing state and allow these images and symbols to evolve and change.

Interpreting Intuitive Images

Interpreting intuitive images, especially those that have to do with love and relationships, requires both the right-creative and left-logical parts of your brain. When you invoke intuitive guidance about your relationships, you connect to personal, subjective energy. Intuitive messages outside your personal realm may be more objective and unbiased. Information that does not affect us emotionally is often easier to receive and interpret.

For instance, if you use your intuition to find out what month a friend's house will sell, you are likely to receive concrete information. You may, for example, get the actual name of the month or its first letter or a season, or perhaps you'll see an image of a specific occasion, like a Fourth of July celebration.

If you elicit intuitive guidance as to what the outcome of a relationship may be, it is likely that you will receive emotionally based impressions. Emotional, subjective, and personal impressions are not always straightforward. There may be no clear yes or no answer. Your information may be, rather, advice for your inner growth, steps to improve the relationship, or insight into the other person's thoughts, feelings, and character.

Images, Symbols, Metaphors

Developing intuitive love is rewarding but can, at times, also be frustrating. Don't give up! Emotional energy can be elusive, difficult to define, and changeable. To add further to the challenges, emotion and intuition speak the same language. They both are powerful energies that communicate through metaphor, symbols, insight, sensations, and vibrations. For this reason, many people do not recognize their own intuitive abilities, because they expect information to come in clear, logical, and linear ways. It seldom does. It takes time and patience to learn to listen, grasp, decipher, and interpret intuitive messages and their meanings.

To understand the meaning behind intuitive impressions, images, symbols, and metaphors, it is necessary to draw upon your inner knowing. Some symbols, colors, numbers, and images have universal interpretations. For instance, an image of the ocean is usually symbolic of collective consciousness, God, or love. The color red is often interpreted as power or active energy. The number three is found in many spiritual practices and may mean magic, intuition, or mind, body, spirit. While it can be helpful to know these common definitions, no one can interpret what you receive better than you can. Even if you don't realize it, you have a personal inner code of understanding that you have worked with all your life. As you develop your own intuitive abilities, you will learn to trust and rely upon that code.

For instance, if I were to ask a group of ten people to imagine a symbol for abundance, illness, or peace, I would most likely get ten different responses.

Intuitive Messages behind Emotion
Sometimes the images that you receive will evoke a particular emotion or feeling. Pay attention and go with it. Don't resist whatever feelings surface during intuitive work.

I sometimes receive intuitive messages in the form of memories. Once while in my car, on my way to a blind date, memories of being in high school kept surfacing. In my mind's eye I saw myself walking down a particular hallway where the "jocks" and other "cool" people congregated. They looked confident and self-assured, and as I passed them I recalled feeling both simultaneously inspected and ignored.

A short time later I was seated across the table from my attractive date, who seemed to be scrutinizing me and at the same time holding back and not opening up or really wanting to get to know me. *Ah-ha!* I thought to myself, *this feels familiar*, as the still-fresh memory of my high school days again flashed through my mind. I realized that this was likely not going to be the kind of connection that I desired.

Interpretation Guidelines
Use the following suggestions as a guideline for interpreting your intuitive-love impressions:

- Assume the beginner's mind. Take the attitude that a wise and loving energy has something to teach you.

- Give the images room to breathe and change.

- Ask your impressions, images, metaphors, and symbols to communicate with you. What do they want to tell you?

- Engage the images in a dialogue. Ask questions one at a time. Ask who, why, how, when? Intuitive information often emerges best with simple, singular questions. Listen for the response.

- Energy is alive. Your impressions have a life of their own. They are not inert objects.

- Trust your initial impressions.

- Use your intuition to interpret. Accurate intuitive interpretation involves both the left and right brain. Allow your thinking mind to suggest an interpretation. Use your right (intuitive) brain to confirm, and get a sense of what feels correct.

- If your image contains numbers, letters, words, or names, use free association to discern meaning. For instance: the number four may indicate four days, weeks, or months. Get an intuitive sense of what feels right to you. Some words and names have literal meaning. For example, if the name *Thomas* appears in your image, this may be the name of an individual who is in some way significantly connected to your question. Names of towns and places like Chicago or the gym might signify these actual places.

- Use your intuitive type to guide you in interpreting the images and symbols. An emotional intuitive can tune in to the emotional feelings associated with images. A mental intuitive can focus on any sudden thoughts or inner, firm sense of knowing. A strategy that works well for the physical intuitive is to hold a crystal, stone, or glass object and imagine it holds the energy of the image. This derives from the practice of using a crystal ball for fortune telling. Once the image is focused inside an object, a physical intuitive has an easier time understanding it. For the spiritual intuitive, asking for help from a spirit guide, angel, or divine being can provide greater meaning to symbols and images.

- Expect to be surprised.

- Know that even if an image seems confusing at first, you will, probably at a later time, receive a flash of understanding.

- Take your time and don't push. Relax and try to enjoy the process.

Formulating the Question

Once you become more confident with your ability to interpret intuitive impressions, you will want to access guidance in every area of your love life. Keep in mind that budding intuitive enthusiasts often overlook the importance of the question. A clear and simple question is the key to accessing specific information. When I give readings, people often tell me to just tell them everything I receive. While I appreciate their confidence in me, a question is like a boomerang. Whatever area or concern you pose to the creative universe will come back to you in direct proportion. Questions open the door for love and wisdom to flow in.

It is best to concentrate on one question at a time and to ask a question that elicits guidance, rather than a simple yes or no. This is especially important for questions about relationships and love, because you will be dealing primarily with emotional energy. Emotional energy is not static or factual, but rather changeable and adaptable in nature. Word your question in a way that will encourage your growth and transformation. You are a work in progress, as are your relationships. When you open yourself to the power of intuitive love, your need to know explicit outcomes will lessen. Instead, you will become more excited by the journey that love has in store for you.

Triangle for Guidance

For practice, we will begin with the question, "What is sabotaging my attempts to attract my soul mate?" Or perhaps, "What can I do to improve my relationship with _____?"

In this exercise and others throughout the book, the symbol of a triangle is used. The triangle is a symbol for the coming together of three spirits as one: your spirit, the spirit of another, and the spirit of love. It is a symbol for the formation of true love.

- Sit or lie down, and begin to take long, deep, cleansing breaths. Breathe in deeply and then exhale, releasing any stress and tension with the out-breath. Focus on your breathing, inhaling relaxation and exhaling stress.

- Bring to mind your question, and repeat it a few times. Feel the increase in energy as you direct your awareness on the question. Continue to breathe and relax. Breathe and come into a receptive and open state.

- Now, using your imagination, create an image of a triangle. Notice as much detail about the triangle as possible.

- Place your question in the center of the triangle. Visualize the words of your question, create a symbol that represents the question, or imagine yourself within the triangle. Do whichever feels most natural to you. Use your imagination, and experiment with the different ways to place the energy of the question inside of the triangle. Notice to which method you feel most connected.

- Now, imagine that outside of the triangle, along the three sides, there are pictures, symbols, and images that represent guidance related to your question.

- You may feel as if you are making this up, and you are. Good job! Actively engage your imagination in creating images. Do not concern yourself with whether or not they make sense. As you receive images, write them down or draw them. Then close your eyes and keep working with the intuitive energy and your imagination.

When you feel as if you have received all that you can at this time, open your eyes and look at what you have written or drawn.

Pick out whatever image or symbol feels strongest to you or catches your interest. Write down any thoughts, memories, or associations you have with the image. Engage the image in dialogue or other communication. If the image had a voice, what would it be saying to you?

Remain loose and open to what surfaces within you. Use your intuition to further interpret the images and symbols.

It may take a few attempts with this exercise before you are able to trust and accept what you receive. This is a new way of doing things. In time, it will feel more natural, and you will find that energy responds to your requests in surprising ways.

Trisha

I did this exercise with Trisha, a businesswoman in her thirties. Trisha felt competent and on top of things in her life, except in the romance department. She had been in a three-year, intense relationship that had ended badly about a year before. She had been sure that the relationship would lead to marriage; instead, it ended with her partner's unfaithfulness. After the end of this relationship, Trisha had not dated. She was afraid of being hurt again and repelled dating opportunities that came her way.

Trisha asked the question, "How can I become excited about dating again?" This is her experience:

"When I closed my eyes and began to relax, I initially felt some stress and anxiety. I do not feel as if I am very intuitive, so I felt like I would fail. I kept breathing, though, and eventually began to feel an increase in energy. As an emotional intuitive, the feelings begin to well up inside. I kept breathing and releasing, and I focused on my question. I suddenly felt an increase in energy, which was surprising. I imagined a purple triangle and saw myself all alone within it. Outside the triangle, I saw a swirl of emerald green and purple circles. I noticed a skeleton on the bottom of the triangle. Its skin was peeling away, but it was not frightening or disgusting, which also surprised me. Instead, bright light came from inside the skeleton. There was a light beam shining all around it. I opened my eyes and I wrote down what colors I observed, and I drew the skeleton.

"With the technique of free association I came to these realizations: The green felt very nourishing to me. I felt like it was telling me to eat better. I realized, as I listened, that I have not had a fresh vegetable in weeks. I did not expect dietary advice, but I knew that it was important for me to take better care of myself.

"When I asked the skeleton what message it had for me, it told me I had to look beneath the surface. It told me that I can open to another person as I gain more information about him. I realized that I always felt as if I needed to be open and vulnerable upon first meeting a potential partner. It seems so obvious to me now, but until this I wasn't aware that I could open slowly in a relationship. I was pushing myself to be emotionally open before I felt safe. I learned a new way to take care of myself. I do feel more excited about dating now."

Practice, Practice

Continue to practice this important fourth step in developing your intuition. In time, you will quickly and easily be able to perceive, tune in to, and communicate with intuitive energy. And don't worry, take all the time you need. Your intuition will never leave you; there will always be opportunities.

4

STEP 4: HOW YOU INTUIT IS HOW YOU LOVE

~~~~~~~~~~~~~~~~~~~~~~~~~~~~~~~~~~~~~~~

Your intuitive type describes how you relate, on an energy level, to others and to your environment. It is also a unique expression of the way you communicate love. Your innate intuitive predisposition plays a determining role in your attractions and love preferences, while it also provides insight into your relationship strengths and weaknesses. Your intuitive type provides a blueprint to experience love's full potential. How you intuit, you will discover, is how you love.

Loving through Your Intuitive Type

Combining the basics of intuitively receiving energy, creating impressions and images from that energy, and interpreting the images through your particular intuitive type will increase intuitive receptivity and accuracy.

The following exercises will help you develop the strength of each intuitive type, even the types different from your own. In them you will tune in to and experience the energy that emotional, mental, spiritual, and physical intuitives experience naturally. You will also be better able to determine your own intuitive type by paying attention to the ease and intensity that you experience while doing each one.

The basic exercise is the same for all intuitive types; however, the focus is different for each. Pay attention to anything and everything that surfaces during the exercises, and always remember to record the experiences in your journal.

Exercise

To begin, think of a person with whom you have a relationship. You can choose the same person you've thought of in the previous exercise, or you can think of someone else.

Sit or lie down, relax, and begin to take long, deep, cleansing breaths. Inhale deeply, and release any stress and tension through the exhale. Focus on your breathing: inhaling relaxation and exhaling stress.

Now, using your imagination, create an image of a triangle. Observe the triangle. What color it is? What is it made of? What or where is its strength or weakness? Tune in to this triangle as deeply as possible.

In the center of your triangle, imagine an image of the person you selected for this exercise. Notice anything you can about him or her. What is she wearing? Note his facial expression and as much detail as possible. Tune in to the person's feelings. What are those feelings?

Tuning in to emotional energy: Imagine a symbol for love. It may be a heart or a red rose or whatever feels natural for you. Imagine this love symbol outside of the triangle. Move the symbol to the inside of the triangle with your person, and at the same time send him or her feelings of love. Notice any changes that take place. Perhaps the symbol or the person will change or transform in some way. New images may appear inside or outside of the triangle. Call on your imagination and tune in to any subtle emotions that arise.

Tuning in to mental energy: Imagine that you can send your person the thought that you would like to understand and know more about him or her. Visualize a symbol for under-standing. For example, a sideways heart that is open or two open, merged hearts is an energy symbol for understanding. Use whatever feels natural for you. Imagine this symbol out-side of the triangle, then move it to the inside of the triangle with this person.

Notice any changes that take place. Perhaps the symbol will change or transform. Communicate to the person inside of the triangle. Ask him or her simple questions, one at a time. Listen, observe, and pay attention to the thoughts that surface, even if they seem to you to be obvious or made up.

Tuning in to spiritual energy: Imagine that you can tune in to your person's aura and energy field. Imagine him or her inside of the triangle, immersed in color. What colors emerge? If the colors are not clear to you, just go with what feels right to you.

Imagine that you are in the center of the triangle with your person, standing side by side. Imagine that your energy changes the colors in the triangle. What new colors emerge when you are together? Tune in to the colors and imagine that they each have a different vibration and meaning. What do these colors each symbolize to you?

Tuning in to physical energy: Imagine your person inside of the triangle, tune in to their physical body. Notice any area of his or her body that feels most intense and places that you are drawn to. Do you sense vibrancy and energy or a lack of vitality? Imagine entering the triangle and standing face to face with your person. How does this feel? Do you feel safe, comfortable, passionate, sexually attracted? Does the person feel connected and comfortable with you? Tune in to your own body. What sensations arise within you?

Record all that you have experienced. Even if it does not make sense, you may want to refer back to what you received for further exploration.

Intuitive Types in Love

Our innate intuition and the way that we love are intertwined. Love, like intuition, is a force that connects and bonds us to one another in mysterious ways.

The Dalai Lama said, "We can live without religion and meditation, but we cannot survive without human affection." Understanding the interplay between love and intuition empowers you with new tools in which to create positive and fulfilling relationships. It gives you insight into the often unspoken nuances of love, and boosts confidence in your intuitive ability.

The path of love for each intuitive type is unique, and speaks to the soul gifts and love challenges that each type must confront.

Emotional Intuitives in Love

Emotional intuitives are in the world to feel, share, and express love. Through the many shades and variations of love's expressions, the bliss, disappointments, the sadness, and the ecstasy, they refine and perfect the power of the heart's lofty potential.

Emotional intuitives naturally absorb the emotional energy of their environment. They are highly empathetic, and without realizing it often mistake others' emotions for their own. Emotional intuitives desire to experience intense heart connections. They long for a soul mate, or a *twin flame*, another who shares their emotional passion, longing, and spiritual aspirations. An emotional intuitive may unexpectedly experience strong and persistent feelings about another and have no idea why or what to do with those feelings. He or she often experiences unexplained waves of emotion while participating in mundane activities like washing dishes or driving the car, or these waves may come suddenly, in the middle of the night. Because of an emotional hunch, this intuitive may call or reach out to a friend or loved one in that person's moment of need or crisis. He or she can, at times, feel overwhelmed by the emotional intensity that comes easily from others and the environment. Emotional intuitives seek to be of service and to heal through their rich inner reservoirs of love.

Emotional intuitives love to love. They fully open their hearts in relationships and expect others to do the same. They can more readily move through the ups and downs of emotions and express caring, forgiveness, and compassion. This intuitive can empathetically feel others' pain and need for support and is able to extend, with complete devotion, deep reserves of love to friends, family, and even strangers.

It is not unusual for emotional intuitives to be drawn to relationships where they can help or heal another. They have a desire to lift others into their realm of pure love, as they hold to the belief that love can heal all. For this reason emotional intuitives must take care to balance their need for deep emotional connections with insight into the other's character and the effect it could have on them. They are too often willing to sacrifice their own well-being in the quest for the ideal love.

An emotional intuitive interacts with absolute love through emotional states of passion, longing, desire, devotion, and self-sacrificing service to others.

It is within the emotional intuitive's soulful quest to fully love that they merge with a greater love and become whole.

To love an emotional intuitive is to accept his or her feelings and emotional intensity, which often cannot be controlled. Express tenderness, care, and compassion, and allow him or her to love you.

Emotional intuitives feel love as:

> Heart opening
> Warmth
> Caring
> Emotional intensity
> Romantic gestures
> Acts of kindness

Laura

Laura stops at the store on her way home from work to buy her boyfriend, Jess, his favorite beer. She knows he's had a hard day. She felt it while sitting at her desk at about 2:30 in the afternoon. Unknown to Laura, Jess was undergoing a work review at that time, and while he sat listening to his demanding boss he imagined Laura there with him. Just soaking in the warmth of her love helped him get through the day.

Mental Intuitives in Love

Mental intuitives live in the realm of thought, ideas, and consciousness. Love for the mental intuitive is truth, plain and simple. It is the key that unlocks the great mystery of life, and it is through loving another that they are able to understand and make sense of life.

Mental intuitives' strengths in loving are understanding, knowing, and predicting patterns and telepathy. In relationships they strive to understand others and desire to be known and valued. They long to be recognized, acknowledged, and fully accepted just as they are. With their natural telepathy, mental intuitives are likely to want to know their loved ones' secret and private thoughts and often intuit them without being told. They can perceive others' patterns of behaving, understand what motivates them, and often predict what a loved one may need and want. To be loved by a mental intuitive is to be exposed. This can either be thrilling and all-consuming or leave one feeling threatened and vulnerable.

A mental intuitive may easily and naturally tune in to the thoughts and ideas of others. They intuit through understanding patterns and the synchronicity of events. They may describe their keen insight into others' motives and behaviors as logic and common sense. Mental intuitives often have the gift of precognition, the ability to perceive future events. They bring into relationships deep understanding, and visionary insight.

Mental intuitives tend to see the big picture in a relationship, and they work hard to achieve their vision of what is possible. Their ability to intuit the mental energy of a relationship can even extend to precognition and the ability to know the outcome before the relationship starts. This future focus means they may lose the magic of being in the moment. A mental intuitive may fail to understand the feeling nature of others and may not be emotionally expressive. Being so tuned in to the mental energy of relationships, these intuitives may miss important cues for tenderness and emotional intimacy. Their expression of caring tends to take the form of questioning and objective understanding rather than warm gestures. They often know much but feel little.

A mental intuitive interacts with love through elevated states of consciousness, compassionate understanding and wisdom, and a desire to teach and enlighten others. For the mental intuitive it is through fully loving another that the truth of life is revealed.

To love a mental intuitive is to appreciate their intuitive, often prophetic mind, and to accept their need to know, understand, and bring meaning to life.

Mental intuitives feel love as:

> Understanding
>
> Communication

Acceptance

Thoughtfulness

Nonjudgmental approval

Recognition for their ideas

Peter

Peter and Natasha have many common interests. They are both curious and intelligent mental intuitives who met at a holistic expo. Natasha was there giving complimentary astrological forecasts, and when she looked at Peter's chart she knew that he was a special man. Since that day several years ago, they have found that the stars are in agreement—each day their love and understanding of one another grows stronger.

Spiritual Intuitives in Love

For spiritual intuitives, love is not just an emotion but a tangible reality. It is energy and vibration palatable to their finely tuned intuitive sensitivities. It is through the journey of love that they are able to perfect and purify the expression of their authentic spirit.

Spiritual intuitives are especially adept at attuning themselves to the vibration of others and perceiving their soulful essence. Thus, they are inclined to receive intuitive information through visions, dreams, and perception of auras and energy fields. They may, for example, dream of a loved one who has passed over and feel comforted and connected to them or may very naturally be able to sense the presence of spirit guides, angels, and ghosts. Unexpected paranormal events are common in the life of a spiritual intuitive.

They are often attracted to others simply because they intuit a connection. This may be the feeling that they have known someone before or the belief that they have spiritual lessons or a specific purpose with that person. The spiritual intuitive will bring to his or her loved ones deep insight, penetrating psychic awareness, and spontaneous feelings of ecstatic union.

A spiritual intuitive may experience a mystical calling to devote himself or herself to a particular person through attractions that may not seem logical, rational, or practical. Spiritual intuitives will often report that they know someone is special to them based on sensations of increased energy, stimulation, and intensity, or by the feelings of bliss and elation they experience when just thinking of someone. Spiritual intuitives can be fun, carefree, and unpredictable in relationships. They can also be a bit confusing and hard to understand. Their spiritual and/or religious life may take precedence over the needs and desires of a partner. For some spiritual intuitives their most significant relationship may be with God, angels, nature spirits, or the Goddess.

A spiritual intuitive can be impulsive, changeable, and elusive. They are likely to end a relationship as mysteriously as it began. They may have a dream or a brief inner awareness that the relationship is over, and that is that. They will simply pack a bag and walk away.

The relationship challenge for the spiritual intuitive is to be in the relationship fully and to commit and communicate to others mentally, emotionally, and physically. They all too often live in their own ethereal reality unaware of their deeper need for intimacy and sharing.

The spiritual intuitive's true desire in love is to break free from the restrictions and limitations of the material world and achieve mystical union. It is paradoxically through their devotion and the sharing of their authentic self to another that they experience true spiritual freedom.

To love a spiritual intuitive is to give him or her freedom, appreciate the spontaneity, and trust that he or she is attuned to an ethereal current of wisdom and truth. Above all else, enjoy the ride!

Spiritual intuitives feel love as:

> Energy
>
> Tingling sensations
>
> Shared purpose
>
> Feelings of connection despite physical distance
>
> Dreaming of another
>
> Love at first sight
>
> Overcoming all odds
>
> Feeling known and appreciated at a soul level

Jim and Mary Anne

Jim and Mary Anne are both spiritual intuitives. They were in love and decided to move from North Carolina to New England. They had planned on getting married first but never quite got around to it. They had also planned to move in September but didn't actually pile all of their things into their car until late November. They had no map, food, or warm clothing. They thought they would buy what they needed on the way.

Why New England? They discovered soon into their relationship that as children they both had dreams of living there. This coincidence was all they needed to make the move.

Physical Intuitives in Love

Physical intuitives have an innate intuitive connection to the three-dimensional world and the physical body. For them love is not ethereal and difficult to grasp. It is real, concrete, lusty, and sensual. For those they love, physical intuitives can move mountains.

Physical intuitives communicate love through touch and have a special gift of healing. These intuitives can soak in the energy of the environment and can unknowingly feel the aches, pains, and physical sensations of others. An example is the father-to-be who gains weight and experiences morning sickness when his partner is pregnant. Physical intuitives often rely on gut feelings and instincts and can pick up intuitive information about others through hand holding, through massage, or simply by sitting close. They often have the gift of *psychometry*, the ability to receive psychic information about others by holding a personal item or photo.

Physical intuitives naturally bond with the physical world and are often drawn to relationships where they feel relaxed, at ease, and where they are easily physically aroused.

These intuitives can perceive the divine in all things and sometimes mistake physical attraction for divine connection. They can be physically demonstrative and highly sexual partners, and they are not always attuned to the silent nuances of love. They need physical demonstrations like touch, hugs, and sex to feel loved. The physical intuitive feels stress when he or she is away from a loved one and may need constant contact to feel connected. They have a strong need to actively participate with their partner, and any activity from cooking dinner together to whitewater rafting will stimulate and strengthen their connection to a loved one.

Physical intuitives love life. They often devote themselves, with unrelenting passion, to those in need and causes and projects that help others. Their love is service and incredible strength in action.

Physical intuitives may unknowingly bond so closely with another that they draw energy from the other person, which may leave that person feeling drained and tired. Their challenge is to express and communicate what they feel and think. These intuitives may have difficulty identifying their feelings and expressing them, as they all too often defer to action and service to express their love. Feelings, love, and emotion can mystify and baffle them, and the idea of spiritually merging with another may be too abstract a concept.

Physical intuitives connect with the higher states of love through awareness of divine beauty, soulful perfection within form, and the transcendent experience of spiritual sexual union.

To love a physical intuitive is to appreciate his or her need for physical demonstrations of love. This may come in the form of help, service, healing touch, or sensual intimacy. Allow him or her to express love to you through physical acts.

Physical intuitives feel love as:

Touch

Cuddling

Walking together in nature

Time spent together

Tangible support and help with chores

Quinn

Gathering herbs on his way home from work, Quinn knows that Jules would welcome a soothing cup of tea after a long day at work. Before entering the front door of their home, he stops to get the mail. There is just one small envelope in the mailbox. He picks it up, and feelings of warmth and laughter come into his awareness. He notices the return address is from their friends, and he imagines that this is an invitation to a solstice gathering. Entering the house, Quinn hears Jules's voice in the bedroom. As he peeks his head in, there is Jules lying on the bed, smiling. Nothing could make Quinn happier.

Types Together

Knowing your intuitive type, and the type of those with whom you are in relationship, deepens intimacy, increases communication, and strengthens mutual acceptance. Relationships give us the opportunity to challenge our preconceived judgments and limiting beliefs about what love is and how it is expressed.

This is what happened for Lynnette when she better understood her husband's intuitive type.

Lynnette

Lynnette is a fair-skinned, thin, sensitive, and gentle emotional intuitive. She called me one day and told me that her husband wanted to meet me for a reading. When Barry came that Saturday morning, he shook my hand assertively, introduced himself, and sat down. When I began the reading I immediately felt the energy and passion of his heart. I told him that he was one of the most focused people I had seen in a long time and that he knew what he wanted. Mind, body, soul, and heart, he longed to serve his country as a medic in the army. He was the perfect example of a physical intuitive. His soul path was one of passionate service.

When I saw Lynnette later, I commented on how her husband was a very heart-centered man. She looked at me with surprise. She had not before considered that his devotion to the service was for him a spiritual and heart-centered path. Lynnette loves art and quiet reflection; spirituality for her is felt in these more poetic and elusive ways. She wanted to feel a stronger spiritual bond with Barry, and knowing that his path is just a different expression of spirituality helped her to feel closer to him.

Your Type Will Evolve and Change

Although each intuitive type experiences and expresses love in distinct ways, you will find that there is a bit of each type within you. Types are fluid, changeable, and respond to our soul's higher purpose in love relationships.

Like most people, I have at one time or another experienced each intuitive type. In daily life my predominant type is spiritual and then emotional. However, in love relationships the emotional intuitive in me takes center stage; and to create balance I consciously adopt more of the mental and physical intuitive tendencies. I will also at times shift into the predominant intuitive type of my partner. When I do this I am able to more clearly tune in to and understand his perspective.

You, too, will find that becoming more aware of the current of intuitive love that silently flows through you will empower you to choose consciously to intuit through one of your less predominant intuitive strengths. In other words, if you are a mental intuitive you may choose to tune in to your physical body and check for intuitive clues, or you might open your heart and feel what your emotional-intuitive partner may be feeling. A shift in intuitive sensing is one way to understand your partner's perspective and consequently increase your understanding of him or her. Remember, perception is reality.

5

STEP 5: LET GO AND INCREASE INTUITIVE RECEPTIVITY

∼∼∼∼∼∼∼∼∼∼∼∼∼∼∼∼∼∼∼∼∼∼∼∼∼∼∼∼∼∼∼

Intuition development is a process of inner refinement, and at some point, no matter what your intuitive type may be, past emotional pain and disappointment will begin to surface. The fifth step in developing intuitive love is to open your heart and release old wounds and negative emotion. This is a natural releasing and clearing-out process that will allow new love and vital energy into your life. When emotional pain surfaces, use it as an opportunity for healing and the deepening of your intuitive ability.

Letting go of what no longer serves you frees your intuition to operate more accurately. Let go of the hurts unjustly inflicted upon you. Let go of the belief that you are not worthy of love or the perception that love is conditional and limited. Open your heart, and just let go. To love you must live in the present.

Unhealed emotional wounds and limiting beliefs send a signal out into the world, attracting similar conditions into our lives. *Like attracts like* is a universal law that is always in operation. (Universal laws define how energy consistently and uniformly shapes and reshapes itself within our universe.) Locked-away pain, resentment, and fear draw people and circumstances into your life that reinforces these emotions. When you are open and accept the good feelings of love, and release the negativity, the universe will respond in kind.

Mistaking Unconscious Emotional Energy for Intuitive Information

Emotional negativity not only attracts negative emotional experiences; it also interferes with your intuitive clarity. When your emotional energy is encumbered with unhealed heavy emotions, the intuitive guidance that you receive will be filtered through this bias. Quite often we mistake the surfacing of unconscious fear and pain as intuitive information. When this happens, not only will the information that you receive be misleading and confusing, it will also likely keep you stuck in the difficult patterns that you might be trying to break free from. This is what happened to Karen.

Karen

Karen, a forty-five-year-old mother of two teenage boys, had been married to Ezra, a software developer, for sixteen years. She had been feeling depressed for several months, and she felt as if her unhappy marriage was to blame. Karen thought her intuition was guiding her to leave the marriage, and she came to see me with the hope that I would confirm she was correct. I was not able to do it. My intuitive guidance told me that the source of Karen's depressed feelings was not her marriage. Her discontent was a signal of the work that she, herself, needed to do. Leaving the marriage would not make her any happier. When I told her this, she seemed both relieved and confused. Karen acknowledged that she had given up on many things in life and felt powerless to make positive changes. I helped her to understand that her intuition could guide her and provide a safe, inner sanctuary during the difficult process of growth. She seemed hopeful and willing to work with her intuition in this way.

The belief that leaving the marriage would solve her problems did not come from Karen's intuition. It was, instead, her feelings of powerlessness and frustration that were motivating her thoughts.

Discerning Guidance from Unconscious Emotional Energy

Being able to discern unbiased and impartial impressions from impressions influenced by hidden beliefs, emotions, and thoughts can be confusing. This is because our thoughts and emotions are energy. It is easy to tap into this energy and mistake it for objective information. This is especially true when we are using our intuition to gain insight and guidance into an intimate relationship.

It has always struck me as interesting that despite what I am feeling or going through in my personal life, I can quickly tune in to a receptive and objective intuitive state when I give readings to others. Yet this is not always the case when I tune in to my personal guidance.

I, like everyone, am biased when it comes to my own issues. I have found that taking a few minutes to clear my mind and emotions before I access my own intuitive guidance makes a big difference in the clarity and objectivity of the information that I receive.

Emotional Energy by Type

There are some telltale signs to which each intuitive type can be alert that indicate the presence of repressed and negative stuffed-away emotions.

For an emotional intuitive there will be an increase in the intensity of emotions and often a build-up of inner emotional pressure. This often shows up as strong and extreme feelings that seem to be out of proportion to the present situation.

A mental intuitive will often have negative obsessive thoughts. If you do not know why you cannot stop thinking about a situation or are stuck in repetitive thoughts, ask yourself what feeling the thoughts are covering up. Obsessive thoughts are almost always motivated by unacknowledged emotions.

A physical intuitive will experience repressed emotions as aches and pains. This may be in the form of headaches, stomachaches, allergies, menstruation problems, or asthma. If you have chronic problems or are tired most of the time, you have old emotions that need to be released.

A spiritual intuitive will feel spacey, unfocused, and ungrounded. They may feel stressed and anxious much of the time, or they may spend an exorbitant amount of time each daydreaming and fantasizing. Releasing emotional energy will help the spiritual intuitive to focus and come back into present time.

Intuitive Meditation

A regular practice of meditation can help to keep the emotional channels clear. Simply sitting and allowing feelings and emotions to surface is all that you need to do to release stuck and negative emotions. Meditation allows the inner intuitive voice to be heard as it stills the mind and brings calm and peace to a stress-filled life. Meditation quiets the constant internal chatter, thus allowing us to connect intuitively with our loving intuitive center.

Meditative quiet can come in many forms. It might be simply closing your eyes, progressively relaxing the body, and focusing on the breath. Often as you turn your attention to your inner intuitive voice, all sorts of sensations, feelings, and thoughts emerge. Sometimes in meditation you receive little in the way of sensations, feelings, or intuitive energy. This is perfectly normal; just pay attention to what you do feel or sense without judging what is happening. As you do this, you will gain more confidence and become more comfortable.

The following meditation can serve as a guide for listening to, releasing, and clearing the intuitive channels. As you feel, listen, release, and disengage from what is not love, you create more energetic space for the pure essence of love.

Heart Flower

- Sit or lie in a comfortable position and imagine breathing and relaxing. Take deep breaths, and send the breath through the body. Then exhale any stress and tension through the out-breath. Continue with this pattern until you begin to relax.

- Allow the breath to move through the body, gently clearing and cleansing any stress and tension you are holding.

- As you continue to breathe and relax, allow any emotions to surface. Do not dwell on what emerges nor allow it to distract you. Pay simple attention to what surfaces, and then let it go. Continue feeling and releasing, allowing the layers of pent-up emotion to emerge. Release what surfaces through the breath.

- When the random thoughts and mind chatter that normally occur in meditation surface, refocus on the breath. Breathe deeply and exhale the tension and stress of your mundane and limiting thoughts.

- Scan your body for any tightness, tension, or stress. Breathe into these areas and imagine the tightness or tension as a ball of emotional energy. Put a name to these feelings, and as you exhale, let go of them.

- Imagine that above your head is a shower of white-light energy. This energy completely surrounds you, cleaning and clearing any negativity in your energy field.

- This shower brings with it revitalizing white-light energy. Breathe it in.

- In this calm and relaxing state, imagine your heart opening. Like a flower in bloom, imagine petal by petal your heart expanding and absorbing love. Through the breath, send this love and compassion all through your body. Imagine this love transforms all negativity, stress, tension, and emotional pain into pure life-giving energy. Continue the gentle, cleansing breath. Release that which no longer serves you.

- Imagine the breath as love moving through your entire body, invigorating and healing.

Sit quietly for as long as feels right to you. Then, when you are ready, open your eyes.

Record your experience in your journal.

Once you've opened yourself to positive and loving feelings, your intuition will become more accurate. Love is life-giving positive energy. Love in its most pure form is not limited by the conditions of time and space. It is naturally psychic, in that it exists everywhere and at all times. When you intuitively tap into love in its most pure form, your intuition will be infused with its vibrant, pure energy.

Absorbing the Energy of Others

Just as it is important to release the emotional energy within you that no longer serves you, it is also necessary to let go of the negative feelings and emotions that you intuit from others. Relationships stir up all kinds of feelings. Not only are we affected by our own emotions, we are also influenced by the emotional energy that we unknowingly intuit from others. Many people, without realizing it, are in a constant state of intuitive receptivity, soaking in the emotions and feelings all around them.

Mental intuitives absorb others' emotions into their own thoughts. For them, intuiting the emotions of another can create a bombardment of ideas and constant mind chatter. The mental intuitive may suddenly have an overwhelming sense of a loved one's issues and concerns, and because ideas and solutions come so quickly and naturally to them, they often, without being asked, offer suggestions and advice aimed at alleviating the situation.

Emotional intuitives can become confused and overwhelmed by the magnitude of emotions that they absorb from others. This intuitive type may become confused about which are his emotions and which belong to the other person. He may experience unexplained feelings about people or places, or may wake up in the night with intense, confusing emotions.

Physical intuitives absorb into their body the emotions and feelings of others. They may feel uncomfortable and anxious when they are close to certain people and even at times become ill. They might also experience a surge of energy when in another's presence.

Spiritual intuitives absorb emotional energy into their energy field. They may dream of others, even those whom they barely know. This happened to me often when I was a child. I remember when I was about ten years old, standing with my mother behind a woman at the grocery store check-out line. Even though we did not know her and did not speak to her, that night I had a confusing and disturbing dream about her.

The emotional energy of others can drain a spiritual intuitive and cause her to feel unconnected to her own intuition and spiritual center. This may even cause the intuitive to become depressed and despondent.

Jenny

Jenny is an example of a caring, intuitive person responding to another's energetic needs. Jenny works in a busy and popular photography studio specializing in wedding and family portraits. Jenny came to see me because she wanted to discuss her career plans. She considered herself an artist, so she took a job at the studio many years ago, to pay for college. But she left school, and instead spends up to ten hours a day photographing children and their families. The studio is owned by Damian, a man to whom she feels confusingly devoted.

When I looked into Jenny's energy field, I was surprised by the tingling rush of potential that jumped out at me. Her soul was like a Technicolor garden of creative possibility just waiting to sprout. I told Jenny what I felt, and she sheepishly told me that she knew what I meant. I told her that in order to make the most of her creative potential, she must spend time away from portrait photography to focus on other art forms. She cried quietly when I said this. She told me that while she knew one day she would pursue her life's passion, she was, for now, devoted to working in the studio. Damian, her boss, had told her often that he would support her going back to school and allow her to work part time. Jenny, however, said she knew Damian needed her to be there.

Her devotion to Damian began years ago as a result of a dream. In this dream Damian reached out to her and told her that he needed her. Jenny woke up convinced that there was a special love bond between herself and Damian, and that for reasons she could not understand fully she needed to be in his life to support him. Ever since then, Jenny said she has felt that Damian needs her. Some days, she told me, she can feel his energy reaching out to her for support and help.

Jenny has been willing to forgo her artistic desire in order to respond to Damian's unspoken request. She feels his emotional needs so profoundly that she cannot imagine leaving her job.

Jenny was not only intuitively picking up Damian's needs and emotional energy, she was responding to it in a way that is not in either one of their highest good. In an attempt to be of help, many loving, caring, and well-meaning people soak up the energy of others and even of the environment. Unfortunately, this does not have the intended effect. It does not help others when you become burdened with their problems, stress, and unhappiness, and it will cause you to feel confused and drained.

How to Know When You Are Being Influenced by Another's Energy
Absorbing the emotional energy of others can be a subtle occurrence. It may take some attentiveness and practice for you to become aware of when you are taking in another's emotions, thoughts, and beliefs.

To know if you are taking in unwanted energy, become aware of feelings like depression, anger, hopelessness, and frustration when in, or soon after being in, the presence of another. Also check your body for sensations like heaviness, tiredness, or listlessness. Are your thoughts scattered and unfocused, or are you worried or anxious when around a particular person? Other telltale signs that you are absorbing another's toxic energy are feelings of being spacey, distracted, or ungrounded, or experiencing a faint internal buzzing sensation.

If you experience any of these sensations and feelings and are not sure if they are your feelings or the feelings of another that you have absorbed, try the following exercise.

Become Aware of What You Are Absorbing
This visualization will help you to become aware of how others affect you and what you may be intuiting from them.

Begin by choosing a person with whom you have a relationship.

- Relax and close your eyes.
- Begin to breathe long, deep, relaxing breaths.
- Now, imagine a circle as clearly as possible. Within the circle imagine a golden orb of light. This orb represents you.
- Relax and breathe.
- Imagine your person as an orb of a different color (red, purple, orange, etc.) energy. Just make it up. Allow this orb to enter the circle with your golden orb.
- Observe what happens. Do the colors merge? Is one more vibrant than the other? Do they connect or repel one another? Does one overwhelm the other?
- Now imagine yourself in the circle with the person. How do you feel? What happens?

- Stay with this energy for as long as possible observing, listening, and feeling.

- When you are ready, open your eyes and record in your journal all that you have experienced.

Abby

My student Abby chose her boyfriend for this exercise. When she visualized the circle and saw herself as a golden orb, she felt light and vibrant. When her boyfriend, as a purple orb, entered the circle, Abby's golden orb seemed to diminish. Her boyfriend's purple orb filled the circle, and she felt over-whelmed.

When Abby visualized herself entering the circle she immediately felt anxious and stressed. She became aware of how she was intuiting and absorbing her boyfriend's worry and anxiety. She realized that she was absorbing his stress about his job situation. He was not happy in his current job and was having a hard time finding another one.

This helped her to realize how much she was being affected not only by her boyfriend's energy but also by the other people in her life.

This realization helped Abby stay internally centered in the presence of others. She became more aware of her tendency to take in others' problems and emotions. Loving others without taking on their feelings was a new behavior for Abby. It soon paid off. She felt calmer and less anxious, and she made it a daily practice to send her boyfriend love and support. They both seemed to benefit from this approach.

Releasing Others

Simply becoming consciously aware that you are being influenced by the energy of others is all that is usually required for you to let go and release whatever it is that you have been intuitively soaking in. Even if you are not completely sure if you are unconsciously intuiting others' aches, pains, thoughts, emotions, or negativity, just focus your awareness within and make the firm intent that whatever energy you have picked up from another be returned to him or her or sent into the purifying energy of unconditional love.

Love yourself and have compassion for your desire to help and take care of others. Imagine that you are being showered with cleansing, white-light love energy, and that the burdens, concerns, and emotions of those who are in your circle of love are lifted and transformed.

6

STEP 6: HARNESS THE POWER OF EMOTIONS

〰〰〰〰〰〰〰〰〰〰〰〰〰〰〰〰〰〰〰〰〰〰

We have just explored how to let go of stuffed-away emotions and the absorbed energy that you may have intuited from others, but what do we do with the ever-constant stream of emotions that are a normal part of relationships? From lust to apathy, compassion to desire, elation to disappointment, and from hope to despair, you have probably experienced some degree of all of these in your connection with another.

To develop deliberate and accurate intuition for use in relationships, we have to deal with emotions—the wonderful romantic feelings and the messy confusing ones as well. The not-so-secret secret of emotions is that they are a powerful form of energy. Learning how to transform the remarkable force of emotions and use them for your highest good is the sixth step in developing intuitive love. Not only will harnessing the power of your emotions benefit your life in untold ways, it will also increase your intuitive potential and accuracy.

Establish a New Relationship
with Emotional Energy

Emotions are energy—useful, powerful energy, which we can harness and utilize. In the realm of intuition and emotions, the old adage "If you can't beat 'em, join 'em" is good advice.

Emotions are an integral part of who we are and what life is. We would sometimes like to eradicate emotions and deny their presence, but this will never be possible. Emotions are indicators that give us information as to who we are and how to take care of ourselves, and insight into the character of others.

You Are Not Your Emotions

The ego-self, that part of you that feels separate and distant from the source of love, easily loses itself in emotions and becomes overwhelmed and powerless. This happens to the best of us. Relationships can invoke intense, deep, and sometimes surprising emotional responses.

When you find yourself trapped in the whirlwind of feeling, try these simple steps:

- Identify what you feel. Put a name to it.

- Fully embrace the potent energy of your emotions. The more you allow yourself to feel your feelings, the sooner the intensity subsides and the emotion passes.

- Become aware that you are not what you feel.

- Recognize that your emotions do not have power over you. You have a choice as to how to respond and whether or not to take any action on what you are feeling.

Psychic Emotional Intelligence

When you align yourself with the potent force of emotional energy, you can actually increase your intuitive ability. Intuitive accuracy depends on your ability to focus and concentrate on invisible energetic impulses without being overly influenced by the chattering mind and emotional ups and downs.

In recent years there has been increasing evidence to support the importance of emotional intelligence. It has been theorized that the emotional intelligence of an individual is as important for overall success in life as other types of intelligence. Emotional intelligence allows one to maintain inner equilibrium despite the prevailing emotional climate, an essential requirement for intuitive clarity and receptivity.

Emotional intelligence describes a variety of emotional skills. Some important aspects include:

- The capacity to perceive and name the emotions that one is feeling
- The ability to perceive what others may be feeling
- The ability to harmonize one's emotions with the environment and with the emotions of others
- The capacity to understand how emotions evolve and change
- The ability to harness emotions to achieve one's goals[1]

Your intuition aligned with these skills make for a potent duo. As you have perhaps discovered, one of the biggest challenges for intuitive accuracy is the ability to differentiate the

---

1. Daniel Goleman, *Emotional Intelligence* (New York: Bantam Dell, 1995), p. 301.

ever-active ego voice from the clear, pure guidance of love. Instead of your emotions interfering with intuitive guidance, they can become an important ally.

The following exercises will show you how to use the force of your emotions to propel you into higher states of intuitive awareness.

Increasing Intuitive Emotional Intelligence

These four exercises will develop and increase your intuitive emotional intelligence. Practice them often to strengthen and refine your intuitive perception.

Stay aware of your predominant intuitive type as you do these exercises, and use the techniques previously discussed for transforming intuitive signals into useful information. The emotional intuitive intuits through emotional energy, the mental intuitive through thoughts, the physical intuitive through the body, and the spiritual intuitive through sensations of energy and vibration and colors. Be mindful of these sometimes subtle intuitive clues, and remember that however your initial intuitive perceptions surface, you can create images, symbols, pictures, or metaphors from them for further guidance.

You may receive only a little clear intuitive information. If so, pay attention to your dreams, daydreams, and episodes of synchronicity. Often, energy information will surface when we least expect it, even days or weeks after we have asked for it. It is likely that during the exercises you will disregard as unimportant certain impressions and information. For these reasons, it is very important to record your experience, immediately, in your journal. Remember that you are your own most reliable source in deciphering the images, symbols, impressions, feelings, inner knowing, and bodily sensations that occur. As you go through the various impressions you receive during each exercise, take time to consider them. Do not rush to interpret. Ask yourself what associations and meaning certain symbols and images have for you. Take care not to overanalyze your first responses.

One quality of emotional intelligence is the ability to harness your emotions in order to achieve your goals. For example, perhaps you and your partner have had recent disagreements and arguments about how to spend and save money. People of high emotional intelligence would take their feelings of frustration and stress with one another and channel these feelings into positive action. They might, for instance, decide to come up with individual budgets and then agree to equally compromise in order to come to mutual agreement on one financial plan.

Transforming Emotion into Awareness
Strong emotions and feelings correctly channeled can heighten and strengthen intuitive awareness. Instead of being intuitively misled and confused by emotions, you can use them to increase your intuitive ability.

Even though this exercise can be done while you are experiencing intense feelings, it is best to use it when you are feeling more calm and balanced.

• Think of a question for which you'd like higher guidance. Write it down. For example:

Will I meet a loving partner?

What can I do to experience more love in my life?

What can I do to improve my relationship with ___?

- After you have written your question down, close your eyes and take a few long, deep breaths—in and out. As you breathe, draw your attention within. Then remember a time in your life that evokes a strong feeling. Recall a memory or event that stirs up emotion. Accept whatever comes to mind. Perhaps it was a time when you were disappointed, excited, elated, or filled with grief.

- Bring to your mind and body the intensity of those feelings. The feelings are not positive or negative; they are just energy. Feel them as energy.

- Next, feel the powerful force behind these feelings. Imagine that this powerful force can easily move through you, releasing any resistance or obstacles that may be interfering with your ability to receive clear intuitive guidance. Instead of repressing the intensity of your emotions and feelings, detach and do not judge them as good or bad. Instead, accept their power and vibrancy. Imagine breathing this energy through your body from the top of your head through the soles of your feet.

- Continue moving this energy through your body, feeling yourself filling with vital and potent energy. Your feelings have now transformed into pure energy. You may feel a tingling or a subtle vibration as this energy moves through you.

- Imagine the flowing energy as a stream of white light, and project your question into it. This white light has intelligence and compassion.

- Listen and receive, become open to whatever guidance comes to you. Maintain this receptive state for as long as possible.

- Use your imagination to create symbols, images, numbers, letters, or words with the energy that you are intuiting. You may experience an instantaneous knowing or a gut feeling. Do not judge or try to think about or understand what you are receiving. Try to remain as open as possible.

- When you have received as much information as you feel is possible at this time, take a few deep breaths and come back fully into your body. Open your eyes, and without thinking too much about what you received, jot down your impressions and information.

As above, take time to interpret the impressions you received, remembering that guidance may not appear immediately. Don't be discouraged if it takes days or even weeks.

Emotional Psychometry

When you have a high degree of emotional intelligence, you are not only able to identify what you are feeling but also what others feel. Then you are able to make decisions that consciously empower and validate those feelings.

For instance, people of high emotional intelligence are often able to detect what their partner is feeling by their partner's facial cues and body positioning.

Intuitive perception takes this skill beyond the boundaries of being able to tune in to the emotional states of those present into the realm of energy. In other words, the person does not have to be physically present in order for you to intuit their emotions and state of mind. With intuitive perception, you have the potential to become aware of someone's emotional state or a situation, regardless of time and space.

The following exercise provides a framework to intuit the emotions and state of mind of another who is not present. With practice it will become easier to differentiate your feelings from the feelings that you may receive from others.

This exercise involves psychometry, the ability to receive intuitive impressions about a person from an object belonging to him or her. It is best to practice this exercise with the items of someone you do not know well. The less you know about the person, the more you will trust the intuitive impressions to be accurate and clear. You will need a personal item belonging to the person—such as a piece of jewelry or a watch, or you can use a photograph of the person. When you feel more confident with your intuitive ability, you can use this technique with someone with whom you are more familiar.

- Sit in a comfortable position and take long, deep breaths— in and out. Close your eyes and take a few more relaxing breaths. Become aware of any thoughts that surface and take note of them. Then, focusing on the breath, let the

thoughts go. Keep breathing and relaxing, and allow any emotions and feelings to surface. As they do, put a name to them. You may feel nervous, excited, doubtful; whatever your feelings may be, accept them.

- Pick up the object or photograph. Hold it, close your eyes, and take a few more long, deep breaths. Feel yourself as a clear and open channel for the feelings and emotions of the object's owner. You are open space, allowing for the entrance of emotional energy.

- Draw your awareness to your heart. What feelings emerge? Breathe into the heart, allow it to open and receive energy. How does this feel? Put a name to these feelings.

- Pay attention to your stomach and your solar plexus. Put a name to the sensations that emanate from this area. Most likely you will sense or intuit more than one feeling. As you put a name to those emotions and feelings, get an inner sense of your accuracy. Does this feel right in your body?

- Breathe into your body, and listen to it. Spend a few minutes breathing and relaxing, and allowing your body to reveal to you any other insights and sensations.

- Hold the object or picture and imagine it can communicate to you. What would it be saying to you if it had a voice? Open and listen; spend a few minutes in quiet receptivity.

When you are ready, write in your journal the feelings, emotions, impressions, or sensations that occurred during this meditation. Use your intuition to help you to interpret what you have received.

Harmonize

Emotional intelligence is also being able to harmonize your emotions with others and with the environment. Say you go home one evening upset about a situation at work that day; your emotional intelligence will allow you to adjust your feelings so you don't walk in and immediately criticize your partner. You would instead be able to enter the house and tune in to the positive mood of your partner.

Intuitive awareness is the ability to recognize your feelings but not be overly influenced by them when tuning in to another. It also allows you to receive intuitive guidance that can positively affect your relationships with others.

Quite often it is difficult to tune in clearly to the energy of a potential lover or partner. Our connections in relationships go through ups and downs, miscommunications, and charged emotions. We can become so immersed in our own experience that we are unable to recognize what others are experiencing. Unfortunately, when we need higher guidance the most to improve or heal relationships, we are often unable to obtain it. This exercise provides a means to connect with another and gain useful, healing guidance.

Harmonizing Your Emotions with Another

Begin by thinking of a person with whom you have a current relationship or someone from your past.

- Think about the circumstances, conditions of the relationship, and connection that you have had with this person. How do you feel about him or her, about the relationship? Are there hurt feelings, confusion, or anxiety associated with your person or with the relationship? Write down all that comes to you, being honest and forthright.

- Once you have written down all that comes to you, sit quietly and take a few long, deep breaths. Now, lie or sit in a position that will be comfortable for you for a short period of time. Close your eyes; take a long, deep breath; and send the energy of your breath to any part of your body that is sore or tense or tight. Breathe in clear white-light energy and breathe out any stress or tension lurking anywhere in your body. Breathe again and let go of any thoughts, worries, or concerns of the day—release and let go.

- As you breathe, imagine that a white-light bubble begins to surround you. You feel the wall of this bubble grow stronger and more protective. It allows only that which is in your highest good to enter. Within the walls of this bubble, allow yourself to release and let go of any feelings and emotions that you no longer need. Feelings of stress, anxiety, fear, pain, and negativity are easily released, and they pass through the wall of the bubble.

- When you feel you have released all that you can at this time, imagine that you can invite into this bubble anyone with whom you would like to improve your relationship. Allow that person's spirit to come close. Offer kindness and compassion. Send him or her the message that you would like your relationship to be healed. Observe the person's energy. Did he or she choose to enter the bubble with you? If you feel resistance, accept it.

- Ask the person's energy to reveal to you whatever he or she would like for you to know. Listen and ask to intuit that person's truth. Keep breathing and listening, paying attention to feelings and sensations that surface within you. Receive the person's perspective. Allow yourself to feel what he or she feels.

- When you feel you have received all that you can at this time, thank the person for sharing his or her energy with you. Imagine that the bubble begins to expand, sending love and harmony to the both of you.

- Harmonize both your energies and breathe in peace and serenity. When you are ready, imagine the bubble dissolving and energizing the both of you. Open your eyes and write down all you experienced.

Emotional Precognition

Emotional intelligence is the ability to understand how emotions evolve and change, and how we can learn from them. It is also the ability to let go of painful emotions from the past and live more fully in the present with an open heart and mind.

You may, for instance, feel angry due to a thoughtless comment from your partner. In time your anger may turn to hurt, and then you begin to feel more sad than angry. Eventually you may be ready to let go of the hurt and move toward forgiveness. You may, then, feel empowered and confident by your ability to forgive.

Intuitive and psychic awareness can provide insight and guidance into how you may need to change and evolve in order to experience the joy and serenity you desire. Some people, for example, are very lonely. Loneliness is a kind of suffering from which it can be difficult to break free because of feelings of powerlessness. Intuitive awareness can help you come into a more positive frame of mind. It can provide you with precognitive perception into a time in the future when you will experience the kind of joy and love you long for. You may also become intuitively aware of a time in the past when you embodied the emotional state you desire. As you become aware that you are experiencing what you most desire, you will be able to move out of the emotionally stagnant frame of mind.

Think of an emotion or state of mind that you would like to change. Possibly you still suffer from a past situation or event. Perhaps you were deceived or betrayed, or maybe you experienced a death or other loss that still causes you distress. Spend some time reflecting on the feelings that you would like to transform. Write these feelings down, even the difficult and disturbing ones. Then think of how you would rather be feeling. Do you want to feel peace instead of anger or acceptance, and hope instead of sadness? Try the following exercise to help you replace negative feelings with positive ones.

- Write down a persistent feeling or emotion that you would like to transform or be free of. Then, sit quietly and close your eyes. Begin to breathe by taking a few long, deep breaths, and imagine tension and stress you feel being released as you exhale. Continue to breathe in, then exhale stress and tension.

- As you continue taking relaxing breaths, scan your body, starting at the top of your head, and draw your awareness to any spot where you notice the emotion or feeling that you are focusing on. Breathe into this part of your body, and imagine you are releasing these feelings and letting them go. Continue to breathe and release.

- When you feel as if you have let go of these feelings as much as you can at this time, draw to your awareness the feelings you would like to feel instead—for example, love, joy, serenity, peace, acceptance. Breathe in these feelings and emotions.

- Imagine a time or a place when you experienced the emotion that you would like to feel. You will probably have the sense that you are making this up, and you probably are. There is a thin line between fantasy imaginings and precognitive extrasensory reality. In truth, you are making up your future, so make it up big! See yourself being loved, living in joy and bliss, forgiving, and surrounded by peace and serenity.

- Observe yourself in an environment that supports your highest good. Make it as real as you can. Imagine the mood, the colors, and the atmosphere. Stay with this image for as long as possible, taking note of the details and the essence. What is happening in this image, and where are you? Are you alone, or is there someone with you? If so, what does the person look like? How far into the future is it? Just allow any information to drift in.

- Then breathe and imagine this image moving into the place in your body where the negative or distressing feelings have been. Breathe this image into your heart, open your heart, and commit to creating a future that supports your highest good.

- Let go of the negative emotions and fill yourself with the positive ones. Imagine yourself filled with joy and peace, as your difficulties have been transformed.

Write down any impressions, sensations, and information that come to you. Take your time with interpreting your impressions. Affirm the positive feelings that you just experienced, and intend to experience them often.

When emotions cease to have control over our moods and actions, an inner calm presence emerges. This is authentic power. True freedom in life is the ability to manage our feelings, thoughts, behaviors, and actions so as attract, manifest, and enjoy love and abundance. Continued practice of the sixth step in developing intuitive love, the ability to transform and utilize your emotions, will empower you to take the reins of emotional responses, no matter how overwhelming they may feel, and use them for your highest good.

7

STEP 7: EMBRACE
ABSOLUTE LOVE

~~~~~~

Love is just love. Or is it? In order to appreciate the connection between intuition and love, we need to understand the difference between relative or personality-based love
and absolute or soul-based love.

Love, in its absolute form, is divine life-force energy and
is at the core of every living being. It is the *glue* of the universe and an electrifying energy. This love is wise, compassionate, and knows no boundaries or limitations. It unifies and
speaks to us of our oneness with all of life. Absolute love draws
distant soul mates to one another and it can heal any wound,
problem, and relationship. Nothing we confront in our lives or
in our relationships is more powerful than absolute love. It is
naturally intuitive in that it transcends time, space, and conditions. When we interact with this love, we ignite the power of
intuition.

Relative love is experienced through the lens of our beliefs,
emotions, judgments, biases, and experiences. We generally

experience relative love in our relationships with others, and it can be clouded by fear and defensiveness. This is the love that disappoints and wounds and yet keeps us looking into the eyes of others, ever hopeful of redemption.

While the source of love that we express to another is personality based, the love that we so dearly seek springs from the soul. The real work of love, then, is to unite us with its pure source and thereby with happiness.

Embracing absolute love is the seventh step in developing the intuition-love connection.

Intuitively Connecting to Absolute Love

I like to ask my clients and friends when they have felt the highest degree of absolute love. Without hesitation most people answer in one of two ways. They tell me that it has been either through their connection with a beloved pet or through a mystical kind of connection in the natural world.

An accomplished artist friend of mine wakes up at four o'clock in the morning one day a week and hikes an hour up a rugged mountain to watch the sunrise. This, he tells me, opens his heart to the love of the universe and inspires him throughout the week.

When you are in the presence of absolute love, despite external evidence to the contrary, you feel that all is well. It is the inner assurance that there is meaning and purpose to your life and that you are loved. You perceive your life as connected to the greater whole and you do not feel alone. We have all had these moments. They come in times of inner quiet reflection, when listening to the gentle song of a rock-laden river, in moments of intimacy with a lover, or perhaps when your cat sits purring on your lap.

An Encounter with Love

Years ago I had an encounter with absolute love that changed me in many ways, not the least of which was an increase in psychic sensitivity. At the time I was working at a community arts council as a part-time art therapist with children who had physical and mental disabilities. The rest of my time was spent as a psychic and medium. I enjoyed both activities, even though sometimes it was difficult for me to keep from psychically absorbing the chaos and distress that often accompanies working with children with challenges.

Determined to bring the healing energy of art to troubled youth, I convinced the arts council to let me start an art program at an alternative school for teenagers who had been expelled from public school because of disruptive or violent behavior. With a big dose of doubt that it would work, they reluctantly agreed. Initially, my time with the students was strained and uneventful. It took many months for them to trust me enough to try and explore what I was offering. Over time the students warmed up to me and began to show interest in both the art and me. I, on the other hand, was experiencing increased anxiety and stress with them. I would go home exhausted and would wake up at night in a state of panic. The aggressiveness and unpredictability I experienced at the school was taking a toll on me. As much as I liked the students, it was becoming harder for me to be in their presence. My psychic boundaries were not strong enough to keep the waves of emotional and mental intensity from affecting me. I thought of leaving the school altogether or stopping my work as a psychic, but I decided to continue with both and to finish out the school year.

One morning as I drove into the parking lot of the school I saw a group of the boys playing basketball. Standing alone next to the court was Rick. Rick was small for his age. He had been born prematurely with fetal alcohol syndrome to a mother who was addicted to alcohol and drugs. His stepfather was violent toward him, and Rick still bore scars on his arm where he had been burnt with cigarettes. Rick entered foster care when he was eight. Now, at age fifteen, he lived in a group home with five other boys. I got out of my car and stood transfixed looking at Rick. I saw his awkwardness with the other kids. He was not very streetwise and was often the focus of cruel jokes and pranks.

As I watched him my heart began to open, not just a little. My heart opened like a dam releasing flood waters. There was a force moving through me, which was not *of* me, and I could not stop it. It felt like love but not the kind of love that I was used to. This was not my love; this was a powerful, intelligent, and kind energy that compassionately loved this boy. I knew that I had to let go of any idea that I could control what was happening. This love seemed to know what it was doing. I continued to watch Rick as he leaned against the rusted fence, and he waved to me. As he did so, I began to see him as a precious and vulnerable boy, not as the angry, potentially threatening adolescent I was used to. I felt feelings similar to that of a mother who for the first time sees her tiny newborn; he looked beautiful. I saw the soul of Rick.

I would have thought that a moment of such transcendence would have happened while I was in a serene place in nature or after a period of intense spiritual focus. But it did not. I was here standing next to a rusted fence, tired, nervous, and just wanting to get through the day.

This event changed me in many ways. The nervousness, anxiety, and stress that had been my constant companion at the school was gone. To say this surprised me would be an understatement. I could walk down the hallways in the midst of tension and anger, unaffected and smiling.

There was a shift in my psychic work as well. The guidance and information that I received after this heart opening was more accurate and clear, and I was no longer exhausted after a session. The number of calls and requests for sessions also increased, and I felt a greater sense of purpose in my psychic work. The love that reached out to Rick was also moving through me and being expressed as psychic awareness.

Sensitize Yourself to Absolute Love

The energy of absolute love can become an integral part of your intuitive ability. Love is energy, and it responds to your intent and will. All you need to do to invoke the power of absolute love is to ask for its enlightened presence. Just open your heart and invite absolute love to flow through you. It is always close and will respond to your request.

The guidance that you receive when your intuition is aligned with absolute love will be creative, uplifting, lucid, and in your highest good. All you need to do to flow with the energy of absolute love is open your heart. Love is everywhere, just waiting for the invitation.

To ensure that your intuition is flowing in the current of this higher form of love, practice distinguishing the absolute love vibration from its more distant cousin, relative love.

Try this. Get into a quiet, receptive intuitive state and ask yourself the following questions. They illustrate the difference between tuning in to your ego-based relative love consciousness and connecting to your soul's wise center of absolute love:

Can I differentiate between my inner voice of wisdom and my constant mind chatter and inner dialogue?

Can I feel the difference between my conditioned emotional responses and the positive flow of revitalizing love?

Do I know when my body tightens up due to stress, anxiety, and fear, and when I am in an expanded and receptive, openhearted state?

Do I know when I am open to higher guidance and when I am drawing from my conscious and unconscious thoughts and beliefs?

There are certain characteristics that will help you to know whether or not you are connecting to absolute love. During meditation, visualization, or contemplation, even when you are being intimate with another, check for these indicators. You may experience these subtle clues emotionally, mentally, physically, and spiritually.

Connecting with the higher vibrations of love will feel:

- Tingling, not flat
- Inspired, not familiar
- Accepting, not controlling
- Uplifting, not confusing
- Light, not heavy
- Expansive, not tight
- Openhearted, not closed
- Generous, not needy
- Giving, not getting
- Stimulating, not draining

The guidance, information, and insight that you intuitively receive when connected to absolute love will open you to new perspectives, new ways of dealing with issues, and motivate you to release negativity toward yourself or others. You will more readily understand the lessons behind your questions and concerns and be inspired to evolve and grow. You will have an awareness of how events are supporting your highest good rather than being concerned about outcomes and getting it right.

Ego-based intuitive information is self-protective, fear based, depends on outer circumstances, and seeks to know information in order to control or manipulate others or conditions. The information that you receive will also be less accurate, often confusing, and less reliable, and may not be of true benefit. Intuition focused in absolute love will provide you with accurate guidance that is positive, healing, and potentially life altering. Intuition that springs from the soul of love will move you out of resistance to change, challenge your limitations, open the heart with love, provide the strength to forgive, and heal suffering.

To connect to the energy of absolute love, you have to remain open to guidance even if it conflicts with your own agenda.

Intuitive Ladder

The following exercise provides a step-by-step format to hone your skills at detecting the subtle energy of absolute love. A common stumbling block for intuitives is not recognizing or being able to trust the origin of the guidance. You may wonder if what you receive is from your own bias and unconscious thoughts or from a higher and more enlightened source. This exercise will help you to detect the difference.

1. Think of one question that has to do with you and a current relationship. For example, "Will my relationship with Sandy improve?"

2. Identify and name your feelings surrounding the question: "I feel anxious and confused by his behavior."

3. Identify what you desire: "I want to be closer to him and to feel positive about our connection."

4. Think of possible answers to your question: "I can talk to him. I can let it go. I can end our friendship. I can wait and see what happens. I can love myself and focus on me. I can see what is happening as a necessary lesson that I need to learn about what love really is. I can pray for us." Consider as many possibilities as you can.

5. Receive intuitive guidance.
   - Take a deep breath, close your eyes, and continue to focus on your breath until you feel relaxed. Release any feelings or thoughts that surface as you breathe.
   - When you feel you are in a receptive state, ask which choice is in your highest good.
   - Continue to breathe. Bring into your awareness each choice, one by one. Pay attention to any physical sensations, emotions, or feelings of increased energy you experience as you imagine each choice.

   See an image of yourself living each choice. How does each look and feel? Tune in to any information that surfaces.
6. Imagine the white light of love surrounding you and your other person. Remember, even if you cannot clearly see white light, your intent is enough.

Depending on your intuitive type, you will pay special attention to those heightened vibrations of subtle absolute love energy that surface through your emotions, your physical body, your sense of inner knowing, and increased sensations of overall tingling and vibration.

Here is how one student recorded her experience in her journal: "As I went through each choice, it became clear to me that focusing on taking care of myself was the best choice. I knew that I had to let go of the relationship for the time being. I knew this because I felt an increase of energy and well-being when I imagined this option. I felt a sense of relaxing peace go through my body, and my heart felt calm. I also became aware that I had attracted this relationship as a lesson to learn how to accept people exactly as they are."

You might not experience as clear a feeling as this student did. You may instead have a sense of knowing, or a symbol or image may surface that reinforces the most positive choice.

Repeat this exercise until you feel confident about the course of action that is in your highest good.

Allow Love to Guide You

Once you can identify, within yourself, the difference between the sensations of absolute love and the sensations of relative love, expect to experience positive changes in your intuitive ability and in your love life. The following exercise will help you to align your intuition with absolute love in order to gain insight into a current relationship and move forward into a positive future.

Love's Guidance Exercise
Start with a question. Think of a single relationship question, and write it down. Use your imagination to come up with a symbol that represents your question.

- Close your eyes and take a few deep, cleansing breaths. Release any stress and tension as you exhale. Continue taking long, deep breaths, then exhaling until you feel relaxed.

- When you are relaxed, imagine in your mind's eyes the outline of a triangle. Notice its color and substance.

- In the center of the triangle, imagine an image of yourself with the symbol and energy of your question.

- Ask for the presence of absolute love to flow through you. Imagine the triangle filling with the heightened vibration of absolute love. Breathe it in and open your heart. Feel this love as a tingling sensation moving up your spine. When you can feel the presence of absolute love, proceed.

- The center of the triangle represents you in the present time. Move your awareness into a receptive state and allow any symbols or images to emerge that represent you in your present-time experience. Pay attention to any sensations or feelings that surface. Stay with the images and listen to them.

- When you are ready, move your awareness to the base of the triangle. This represents the past energy surrounding your question. Allow any images, symbols, information, feelings, or sensations to emerge. Ask for inner guidance about what you need to release from the past.

- When you are ready, move your awareness to the top of the triangle. Imagine that this area represents the future energy of your question. Open yourself to the presence of absolute love. Ask for guidance that is in keeping with the highest good. Pay attention to any symbols, images, feelings, thoughts, letters, words, or sensations that emerge. Stay with this and allow it to change and evolve.

When you are ready, open your eyes, and, in your journal, write down everything that you just experienced.

Jen

Jen came to see me because she was anxious and concerned about her marriage and her future. She did not know what to do or where else to turn. Jen is in her late twenties. She has been married to Rex for four years and has a young son. She works nights and goes to school during the day. Her life is busy, and she seldom has time to just sit and relax. Jen said she recently has begun to sense that her husband is no longer in love with her. As we got deeper into the session, it became apparent to me that there was another man in Jen's life. When I asked her about it, she readily confessed that she had been secretly meeting a male co-worker. She told me she knew she had a problem with fidelity, and she felt very guilty for seeing the other man. She said she was not worthy of Rex. He was a good man and he deserved better. Although she still loved Rex very much, she felt as if she should end the marriage.

Jen wanted guidance and insight into her relationship with Rex, and so I led her through the triangle exercise. Here is what Jen learned:

In the center of her triangle Jen saw herself. The center was dark, and she was standing next to a small, muddy lake. There were dark clouds in the sky, and she was shivering. Jen felt sad. She also saw a golden ring or circle in the sky. She kept reaching for it. Her grandmother, who had died several years before, was also there; she seemed to be leading Jen to the bottom of the triangle.

At the base of the triangle Jen saw the house where she'd grown up. Big red splotches kept appearing. She heard her father's angry voice, and she saw herself in her backyard looking at the sky.

When Jen moved to the top of the triangle, she felt light colors of pink and gold. She felt the presence of angels. Her body relaxed, and she felt the tingling sensation of love comforting her. She then saw the letter *A* and an image of a plow and fields of newly planted flowers. She felt a sense of peace.

When Jen finished, I asked her to interpret what she received. She seemed a little nervous, but I told her just to give me her impressions and to trust in her ability to discern the meaning. She said she was, at first, surprised with how strong and vivid the images were. She knew that the dark sky and clouds in the center of the triangle represented her confusion. She felt as if the lake represented her emotional energy; it was muddy. The golden rings in the sky were her belief that happiness in her marriage was beyond her grasp. When her grandmother appeared she felt comforted, because Jen loved and trusted her grandmother. She knew that her grandmother was leading her into important information to help her understand her own behavior and feelings.

At the base of the triangle Jen became aware of the home she'd lived in until age ten. This was the time before her parents divorced. Her father was a heavy drinker and prone to fits of rage and anger. The color red represented the fear and anger that she still felt. Jen knew that she had to let go of this in order for those past wounds to heal. When she saw her younger self looking at the sky, waves of compassion moved through her. She remembered praying to the angels to take her with them.

Jen then moved to the top of the triangle with the angels. They lifted her into a higher vibration, just as they did when she was a child. Jen started to cry when she felt their love. She knew that the angels were telling her she needed to *plow* her way through her past issues. She knew that the flowers represented her positive growth. There were fields and fields of beautiful flowers. She knew that there would be much love in her future. At first, she thought that the letter *A* represented adultery, but that didn't feel right. Instead she interpreted it to represent the month of April. This was the month of her wedding anniversary, and she knew that she needed to work on her marriage. The peace she felt would come as a result of her own healing.

Jen is a mental intuitive, so much of what she received came to her through an inner sense of knowing and understanding. Information seemed to pour into her awareness when she focused on the images and symbols. She was also able to trust her accuracy in interpreting the images and symbols by the feelings of confidence and inner assurance that occurred when she gave meaning to the various inner pictures.

Practice the seventh step in developing the intuition-love connection, consciously invoking the presence of absolute love whenever you engage your intuition. In time you will naturally open to this powerful current of love energy, and not only will your intuition blossom but your love life will positively transform.

8

STEP 8: EXPERIENCE YOUR LOVE ENERGY

Y ou are love. I know that this might seem like an elusive and mystical concept. But it is not. I often experience people in this way when I tune in to them in intuitive readings. Even if they have come into my office skeptical and grumpy, as soon as I begin to focus on their energy I feel love.

Despite the difficulties and challenges that you confront, you are a powerful being connected to the current of absolute love. Knowing yourself as love often begins with knowing yourself as energy.

Experiencing yourself as love energy is the eighth step in developing the deliberate intuition for use in your relationships.

Know Yourself as Energy

The physical body comprises millions of tiny cells, which are constantly in motion. Even though we appear to be solid, our physical bodies are in a continual process of growth and decline, as cells change, die, and are born each microsecond. The body is a network of miraculous, interwoven, and complex energy. We are energy so multidimensional that we can barely comprehend it, and we scarcely have language to describe it.

Surrounding each person's physical body is an aura or energy field. This electromagnetic field is visible with the use of Kirlian photography, which can capture the aura's various vibrational colors. Within this complex web of energy are swirls of energy, referred to as chakras—the Sanskrit word for circle or wheel. The energy field contains seven major chakras, which are vertically aligned and extend from the base of the spine to the top of the head. Each chakra has a spiritual-intuitive function. Just as our organs all have specific functions to keep the body healthy, so the chakras each have a role in our well-being. There are many books that describe the chakras in detail. We will briefly describe them here and how you can use them in meditation to help develop your own language for love.

Each of the seven chakras is able to receive the pure energy of absolute love. Each has an energetic love frequency that can either promote or stifle the ability to give and receive love.

Through the seventh or crown chakra, located above the head, love is expressed as an inner sense of connectedness to divine love and the ability to feel the presence of angels, loved ones in spirit, and benevolent spiritual helpers. This is the chakra through which spiritual intuitives most often receive intuitive energy information.

The sixth chakra, located in the center of the head, is sometimes referred to as the *third eye*. Through the sixth chakra love flows as divine intelligence. It contains mental energy, thoughts, beliefs, and the spiritual gift of clairvoyance. Mental intuitives are most comfortable intuiting through this chakra.

The fifth chakra, located in the throat, is the chakra of self-expression and will. Love flows through this chakra as mutual sharing and nonjudgmental acceptance of oneself and others. Through the fifth chakra, we are encouraged to communicate authentically with others and with the world.

The fourth or heart chakra receives energy as emotion and feeling. Love in this chakra is expressed as infinite abundance and compassion. The fourth chakra receives and expresses love in all of its variations. The emotional intuitive primarily intuits through this chakra.

The third chakra is located in the solar plexus. Love flows through this chakra as compassionate power and the ability to love and take care of one's self. Physical intuitives are most likely to intuit through the third, second, and first chakras.

The second chakra, located below the belly button, expresses love in creative action. It holds the energy of our finances, sexuality, relationships, and creativity. This chakra expresses love as sensuality, sexuality, kindness, and generosity.

The first chakra, located at the base of the spine, corresponds energetically with our connection to the physical world. Love flows through this chakra as physical energy, stamina, and courageous commitment to choices that enhance the life of all living beings.

Our energy body and our chakras are like flowers that open and receive the positive, life-giving flow of love. We energetically reach out to others in our environment and our multidimensional self in order to give and receive this love. Intuition is the faculty we have all been given with which to understand and increase the life-sustaining flow of pure love that is always available to us.

Ask yourself these questions; they will give you insight into how your chakras are operating in relationships:

1. Am I able to feel the presence of love, regardless of my relationship status?

2. Am I able to discern the purpose and lessons inherent within my relationships?

3. Am I able to express my truth to those I love?

4. Does love, not fear, motivate my relationship decisions and choices?

5. Am I comfortable expressing love as compassion, not control and manipulation?

6. Am I comfortable with expressing love as passionate sensuality?

7. Do I demonstrate my love to others and the world through acts of kindness, service, and devotion?

Developing Your Intuitive-Love Vocabulary

Your inner, intuitive voice can help you to tune in to the different expressions of absolute love. In the following exercise you will work through each of the seven chakras with your imagination to create images and symbols to help you define and relate to love. Trust what surfaces. We already have a well-developed symbolic inner code of understanding, and intuition simply helps us to become more conscious of it.

Seventh Chakra

- Close your eyes and begin to breathe long, deep, relaxing breaths. Allow any thoughts and emotions to surface as you breathe. Take note of them and release them as you exhale. Continue to breathe and release any tension or stress.

- When you feel relaxed, imagine that there is a gold swirl of energy above your head. Imagine that you can breathe in love, as divine energy, through the top of the head.

- Keep breathing and allow an image to emerge that represents love as divine energy. This might be a symbol, object, color, or cartoon-like picture. Accept what emerges, and keep breathing.

- Open your eyes and draw or write down what you received in your journal.

Sixth Chakra

- Close your eyes and continue to breathe and relax. Imagine a swirl of purple energy surrounding your head. Imagine this energy as love expressing itself as wisdom. Breathe this love in.

- Keep breathing and allow an image to emerge that represents love as wisdom. This might be a symbol, object, color, or cartoon-like picture. Accept what emerges and keep breathing.

- Open your eyes and draw or write down what you received in your journal.

Fifth Chakra

- Close your eyes and continue to breathe and relax. Imagine a swirl of blue energy surrounding your neck and shoulders. Imagine this energy as love expressing itself as self-acceptance. Feel this love and breathe it in.

- Keep breathing and allow an image to emerge that represents love as self acceptance. Accept what emerges and keep breathing.

- Open your eyes and draw or write down what you received in your journal.

Fourth Chakra

- Close your eyes and continue to breathe and relax. Imagine a swirl of green energy surrounding your heart and chest area. Imagine this energy as compassionate love. Feel this love and breathe it in.

- Keep breathing and allow an image to emerge that represents love as compassion. This might be a symbol, object, color, or picture. Accept what emerges and keep breathing.

- Open your eyes and draw or write down what you received in your journal.

Third Chakra

- Close your eyes and continue to breathe and relax. Imagine a swirl of yellow energy surrounding your waist and solar plexus. Imagine this energy as power. Feel this love and breathe it in.

- Keep breathing and allow an image to emerge that represents love as power. Accept what emerges and keep breathing.

- Open your eyes and draw or write down what you received in your journal.

Second Chakra

- Close your eyes and continue to breathe and relax. Imagine a swirl of orange energy surrounding your lower body. Imagine this energy as creative action. Feel this love and breathe it in.

- Keep breathing and allow an image to emerge that represents love as creative action. This might be a symbol, object, color, or cartoon-like picture. Accept what emerges and keep breathing.

- Open your eyes and draw or write down what you received in your journal.

First Chakra

- Close your eyes and continue to breathe and relax. Imagine a swirl of red energy surrounding your hips, legs, and feet and connecting you to the earth. Imagine this energy as oneness with all of life. Feel this love and breathe it in.

- Keep breathing and allow an image to emerge that represents love as oneness with all of life. Accept what emerges and keep breathing.
- Open your eyes and draw or write down what you received in your journal.

When you have gone through each of these exercises, contemplate the symbols and images that you have recorded. It is not necessary that you completely understand what you received. You can meditate on each one of these symbols and further develop your inner intuitive-love vocabulary. To understand further and learn from these symbols, allow them to communicate to you. Even if you feel as if you are making the impressions up, trust that they have a message for you. Keep working with the energy; eventually you will sensitize yourself to the various expressions of love energy and become more confident in interpreting what you intuit.

You can draw on the symbols that have emerged in this eighth step of intuitive-love development in future intuitive work, to guide you in interpreting and understanding the energy you might be receiving.

9

STEP 9: WELCOME TRANSFORMATION

〜〜〜〜〜〜〜〜〜〜〜〜〜〜〜〜〜〜〜〜〜〜〜〜〜

Love-focused intuition is more than just information gathering. It is an invitation to transformation that is change on a deep and profound level. This is not "trying to change" or struggling with issues. Instead, it is the graceful opportunity to move beyond our limitations, our boundaries, and our unconscious patterns. As you transform, your relationships become infused with positive energy.

The ninth step in developing intuitive love is to accept that as you explore and develop the intuition-love connection, you will change, evolve, and transform.

Intuition is a catalyst for transformation. An intuitive thought or idea, emotional healing, or a persistent message brings with it new and spontaneous awareness. Even though the insight may seem impractical or illogical, it inspires you to shift perspectives, change your attitude, and grow beyond your comfort zone.

At times, you may try to ignore or quiet the intuitive knowing, because it runs counter to the way that you've been doing things or it conflicts with how others perceive you. Yet this is exactly the time to seize the moment. It is often those persistent, illogical messages that are the most potent.

Deepening the Intuitive Process

With intuitive insight come increased options. Once we know something we always know it, and we are forever changed. New choices, opportunities, and decisions naturally unfold from increased awareness.

Intuitive insight can transform a stale relationship, bring hope where there is despair, provide insight into unconscious patterns of behaving, heal emotional wounds, and lift us into joyful love. Intuitive awareness sets us free to create the kind of relationships we desire.

Integrating intuitive information into our lives is a process. Although inner guidance may provide the solution to a problem or the foretelling of an event, the deeper work of change often comes through a progression of intuitive insights.

Promoting Transformation

This four-step exercise incorporates the intuition basics and includes the use of visualization to promote transformation.

1. Set Your Intention

Think of a relationship you would like to transform, or a behavior or negative pattern within yourself that you would like to change or heal.

Write down your concern in detail. What emotion or feelings does this invoke in you? What would you most like to change? Imagine the feelings and emotions that you would like to be experiencing. Intend to create anew.

2. Intuitive Visualization

- Find a comfortable and quiet place to sit or lie down, and close your eyes. Begin to take in long, deep breaths. Inhale deeply, feel your body energized and relaxed by the breath. Feel the breath circulate throughout your body. Exhale and release any tension or stress.

- Imagine an expansive, open desert-like place in nature. Deep hues of reds, oranges, and browns grace the landscape. Shadows of falcons, flying high overhead, stretch across vast rocks and hills. A warm breeze helps you to feel relaxed and at peace. You are reminded of all that is good in life.

- You notice a path leading into a barren canyon. You follow the path and notice the sun setting in the distance. The path leads you past rocks and boulders that are dark red and varying shades of brown. As you enter the quiet canyon it is dusk, and you notice the rising crescent moon.

- In the center of the canyon there is a massive rock plank with a bonfire slowly burning on top of it. You are drawn to the bonfire. It is warm and energizing. The bonfire is here for you, and it needs fuel. You can throw into it any feelings, past events, limitations, and unsatisfying experiences that you no longer need or want. Take your time and imagine tossing into this bonfire anything that no longer serves you. Even if you can't be clear about all you feel, imagine putting all of the energy into a bag and throwing the bag into the fire.

- When you have released all that you can, watch it burn. The fire burns away all of the old energy. Watch as the bonfire dies down to ash, and allow the smoke to clear away.

- From the ashes a new energy is now ready to emerge. Using your imagination, create an image that represents the new energy coming in to your life. This could be an image of you in the future or a symbol or object that signifies a desire coming to life. Once we release the old, we make room for new levels of intimacy, satisfaction, experiences, people, and opportunities.

When you are ready, open your eyes and write down or draw the image, symbol, or object, and any impressions that you received.

3. Discern the Message

Meditate or sit quietly with the symbol or image that you have received. Write down any associations, thoughts, or ideas that come to you. You may not feel as if you are receiving clear information, but try not to get frustrated. Keep in mind that it is only your thinking self that becomes confused; the deeper, wise part of you is not confused.

Allow this step to evolve over time. Sometimes you will have immediate awareness of the message but not always. Use your intuition and common-sense logic together to interpret your impressions.

4. Act on Intuitive Promptings

Take action to reinforce the new behaviors, opportunities, and experiences coming your way. Transformation always requires your participation. Practice listening, interpreting, and then taking action on what you receive. A curious quality of working with your intuition is that it often does not make sense and it is not always logical. Yet acting on intuitive prompting opens the door to surprising new energy. Intuitive love is creating from absolute love, and it does not adhere to the rational and the probable.

For instance, perhaps your hope is that your partner treat you in a more loving and kind manner. Let's say that the symbol you receive during the meditation is that of a white dove. You contemplate the image of the dove, and feelings of peace and purity emanate from it. You take this to mean you will soon experience peace in the relationship. On your way to work the next day, you drive by a bookstore and feel drawn to go inside. You respond to this intuitive prompting and go into the bookstore and wander up and down the isles. In the self-help section, you notice a book with the image of a white dove in flight on the front cover. You pick it up and see that it is a book on improving communication in relationships. You buy the book and find in it a section with helpful suggestions about the same issues you have in your relationship.

Sometimes a simple intuitive awareness is all we need to transform. I rely quite a bit on intuitive guidance in my relationships. I am sometimes embarrassingly blind to my character defects and what I intuitively sense surprises me. Just recently, I received the inner message that I was acting defensively and needed to open my heart and trust that I could expose my vulnerabilities. When this inner awareness emerged, it was a little surprising and humbling. I thought my heart was open . . . yet as I sat and allowed the message to unfold I realized that I was often defensive with others for no reason. My heart was open but only conditionally. This awareness inspired me to pay more attention to my unconscious protective attitude and open my heart. It paid off. Besides the beneficial effect that it had on my relationships, breathing and opening up feels much better than closing down.

One of the most important if difficult aspects of consciously working with intuition is becoming comfortable with not knowing. This may seems like a paradox, since we develop our intuition as a means to gain information. Yet intuition that is of true benefit will always nudge you a bit into the unknown. It is not always easy to recognize our own behavior and break emotional patterns. Even when it logically makes sense to change them, our old protective, safe ways of operating do not let go so easily. Remember though that the wisdom and compassion of absolute love always have your back. Intuition connected to love is a trustworthy guide, and although transformative change may be challenging, the rewards are forever.

Intuitive Love at Work

The story of Arlene is an example of the healing and transformative power of intuitive love. Even when there appears to be no solution or way out of difficulties, intuitive love finds a way. I first met Arlene when she was considering divorcing her husband. She came to my class with her friend, and although she had little experience, she took to intuitive work very naturally.

Soon after the class, she came in for a private session and I learned that her husband, Ted, a successful banker, was rarely home, and when he was, he was often grumpy and demanding. Arlene told me that many of her friends envied her life. Ted was successful and provided her with a comfortable lifestyle. She never told her friends of his quick and piercing temper or how he could go on a verbally abusive tirade for no apparent reason. Arlene said Ted often insulted her by calling her names and would even push and shove her, if he was in a particularly bad mood.

Arlene felt trapped. She had never worked outside the home, and she didn't have close family for support. She didn't know where to turn. Because of the calmness and peace that she felt during the meditations in the class that she took with me, she decided to commit to developing her intuition, specifically to help her in her marriage.

She practiced meditation every morning after Ted left for work. She took to it quite well and told me that within a few weeks of beginning, she could feel a subtle, warm presence as soon as she closed her eyes and took her first deep breaths. She looked forward to the loving and comforting presence that seemed to greet her each day.

Slowly her meditations began to change. The subtle loving presence became stronger and more tangible. She felt that this loving and persistent presence wanted to communicate to her and help her. She knew that she could allow it to enter her heart, but she resisted. Finally one morning she took a deep breath and opened her heart. What at first felt like slight warmth was now stirring up the deep feelings of anguish and hurt she had been stifling for many years. Even though allowing these feelings to surface was so very difficult, she felt better afterward and so she continued the process.

As Arlene's meditations progressed, she trusted this quiet presence more and more. Arlene is primarily a spiritual intuitive and naturally took to tuning in to the unseen, ethereal energy. She soon began to identify the presence that she felt as her guardian angel. She called the presence Mira, after the heroine in a childhood fairy tale. In time, she began to see Mira as soft, shaded colors of turquoise and pink, and she began to be able to decipher the images and symbols that came to her during her meditations. She also began to hear Mira's faint voice gently guiding her.

Over the course of several months the voice became clearer, and Arlene became more adept at communicating with Mira. She wrote down the messages and began to act on them whenever possible. The guidance she received led her to heal and improve her self-perception and make positive choices in her life. She told her friends the truth about the difficulties that she was having with Ted, and she joined a support group for women in abusive relationships. She also enrolled in a medical transcription course at a local college.

Arlene's sense of self-confidence and inner strength grew, but Ted did not seem to notice. In spite of all her work, Arlene still did not know how to make changes in her marriage, and leaving Ted still seemed impossible to her.

One evening, Ted came home from work early and began to pack a suitcase. Arlene thought he was just on his way to a business meeting. Ted didn't say a word when he left. When Arlene went to the bedroom she found, instead of the usual packing mess, a folded note on her night table. In the note, Ted told Arlene that he was leaving and that he wanted a divorce. He gave no further explanation.

Arlene felt a huge weight lift off of her shoulders, and she felt unexpectedly positive about her future. She smiled and thought of Mira. Dear Mira, she thought, thank you, thank you. She knew in her heart that this was a blessing and she felt the loving inner confidence that everything would be okay. She felt no fear, no dread, and the inner assurance that she could take care of herself; this she thought was a true transformation.

The Gift of Change

Intuition offers a cushion of safety that helps us feel our inter-connectedness with all of life. It helps us to get in touch with the powerful forces of love and healing that reside within us all and to draw strength and support from them. This ninth step, accepting transformation, will empower you to embody these powerful forces of love and therefore attract passionate and satisfying love relationships.

There is divine plan at work in your life. Even if you have been hurt or disappointed or do not understand the purpose of a particular relationship, you can trust that love's current is forever moving you in the direction of bliss and unconditional love.

Congratulations! You have moved through the nine steps of developing intuitive love. I encourage you to review the steps often. Some may take longer to master than others. This is a lifelong journey which will require you to grow, evolve, and learn more about yourself, others, and love. The next sections will show you how to put your intuitive-love ability into action.

PART II

*Use Your Intuition to Heal
and Transform Yourself,
Others, and Your Relationships*

10

CREATING HEALTHY
INTUITIVE BOUNDARIES

~~~~~~

Have you ever tried to have no thoughts or no feelings? We all know how impossible this would be. Turning off your intuition is similar. You can ignore it, but you can never really shut it off. To use the intuition-love connection in your everyday life, it is important to establish clear and safe personal boundaries or you may become overwhelmed by the constant stream of intuitive energy coming your way.

Like your other senses, your intuition is always at work and can often surprise you. For instance, your intuition can unexpectedly bombard you, while standing in line at the local coffee shop, with all kinds of information about the quiet, attractive stranger in front of you. You might wake up in the middle of the night from a disturbing dream of your boyfriend kissing another woman, or when your partner leaves the house telling you that she is going to the store, you might have a strong suspicion that she is not telling you the truth.

Intuition can fill in missing spaces about another's character, personality, and intent. It can also answer questions that you have not asked.

Unfortunately, intuition is not always obvious and easy to decipher. Even though it is always able to provide us with guidance, its message can quite often be difficult to discern. The more you use your intuition, the more likely it is that you will receive unprompted information about another or about conditions and events beyond your control. You might not always understand why you received certain intuitive messages and struggle to know what to do with them.

Learning how to integrate your intuition effectively into your everyday life can be both rewarding and challenging.

Unsolicited Intuitive Information

We continually connect, receive, absorb, and respond to the energy of others. Communication is verbal, but it is also energetic. Your intuitive sense is as much a part of your overall functioning as is your sense of taste, smell, hearing, sight, and touch. You cannot turn your intuition on or off, but you can shut down your awareness of it and deny its existence.

When you repress intuitive awareness, it doesn't go away. It instead surfaces in confusing and perplexing ways. Emotional intuitives may, for example, feel waves of emotion or receive random feelings that seem to have no connection to themselves or their current situations. Consistent and unproductive thoughts about another's problems and issues may plague the mental intuitive. The spiritual intuitive may have incomprehensible dreams about a partner or about a distant friend. A physical intuitive might absorb others' energy into his or her own body, and consequently experience increased levels of stress, anxiety, or illness.

Working with Spontaneous Intuitive Insights

Spontaneous intuitive impressions are not always easy to recognize and decipher. This is especially true for impressions we receive about relationships. It is often easier to deal with intuitive information that concerns our own lives than it is to know what to do with the impressions that we receive about others. It can be unsettling to receive guidance for or about another without apparent logic or purpose for receiving it. These kinds of intuitive insights often occur unexpectedly and unbidden.

When we receive unsolicited intuitive information and guidance for another, many questions may surface. Do I share the intuitive insight? Is there a reason that I tapped into this information? Why was I meant to know this? What if the impressions are inaccurate or we misread or misinterpret the guidance?

Here are some guidelines to help you interpret and share intuitive information with others:

1. Listen to and write down your dreams, gut feelings, empathetic impressions, and intuitive thoughts as well as moments of clear knowing, precognition, and insights. Do not discount or ignore anything.

2. Do not jump to conclusions. Discerning the message of an intuitive insight may require time and patience. Consider that your intuitive insight may be telling you something about yourself and not the other person in the

relationship. For example, dreaming that your partner is having an affair might be telling you that your partner is being dishonest or it may indicate your own insecurities and fears. Perhaps you have an unconscious concern that you will be abandoned or that you are not worthy of a good relationship.

3. Be honest with yourself. Spend time in quiet reflection and journaling. Be willing to explore your fears. What might your intuitive impressions be trying to tell you about yourself?

4. Ask for guidance before you share your insight with the other person. Is it in his or her highest good to know this information? Ask that the person provide you an opening to share your advice or insight. Then, if you feel it is right, share your impression, being honest and forthright. Communicate your impressions clearly and openly. Be willing to talk with the other person without judging or offering advice. Simply express what you have received and know that the rest is up to him or her. You cannot force guidance on anyone.

5. Be prepared for the other person to deny your intuition, even when you are sure of its accuracy. This is likely in situations of infidelity, deception, or other untruthfulness. If this happens to you, pay attention to outer cues that either reinforce or invalidate your intuitive impressions. If your impression indicates infidelity, for example, look for cues in your partner's appearance and actions. Has he traded his faded jeans for freshly pressed pants? Is

she eating healthier foods and working out more? Does he hide the e-mail or website he's looking at when you enter the room?

6. Ground your intuition with practical steps to reinforce what you know to be true. It can be very distressing when your intuition is met with denial or its accuracy ridiculed.

7. Meditate, go within, and ask to be guided about how to take care of yourself. Then, act on your own highest good.

8. If you receive random information or insight into someone you do not know, visualize them in loving white-light energy. Quite often the spirit of those in need unknowingly seeks out the energy of loving and open people.

Clarity of Intent

As you focus more attention on your innate intuitive ability, it will begin to intensify, and there will likely be an increase in the magnitude and variety of your experiences. With increased intuitive awareness comes responsibility, to yourself and to others.

Knowing what to do with your intuitive impressions is not always simple and obvious. Eventually you will only consciously receive as much intuitive information as you are able to work with. Without realizing it you will ignore and repress your intuition if you are uncomfortable with what you sense.

The best way to increase intuitive receptivity is to have a clear intention of how and where you will use your intuition. When I first began full-time psychic work, I would often be overloaded with information, impressions, and sensations. I often struggled to accurately relate the information to my client. Sometimes when I felt particularly accurate, the information was not useful or positive. I would see the disappointment or concern reflected in my client's eyes. I began to understand the power that intuitive information can have over a person's life and the responsibility that it demands. With this realization came my decision to begin every session with the prayerful intent that I only receive information and guidance for the person's highest good. While being an accurate intuitive may be exciting work, the ability to align with the realms of love and wisdom, and provide ourselves and others with this level of insight, is of much greater benefit.

Love combined with intuition can be a tricky business. Become conscious of how you would like to use your intuition. Recognize the power that you have to affect the course of your life. It can be tempting to want to use your insight and will to suit your own needs and desires. Ask for guidance that will further the highest good for all concerned. This simple intent can make a vast difference in the quality and scope of the information that you receive. Remember, the intuitive's role is simply to express the truth and leave the choice to others as to how they receive and act on the guidance.

Living an intuitive, openhearted life is a courageous act. When you open yourself to the power of absolute love, you become a beam of light to others. They will be drawn to you by the force of love that moves through you.

Intuitive receptivity often induces intense emotional states, which attract highly charged, passionate relationships. Because of the intuitive's strong energetic current, he or she attracts others who are in need of guidance, help, or support. Sometimes this attraction is mistaken for love.

Kaly

Kaly, a kind and gentle social worker, dated Bret for over two years. They had known each other in college but hadn't been in contact since. Just a few months before they met, Bret's wife of many years had left him for another man. A few weeks after that, he lost his job. About this time, Bret ran into Kaly at a mall. They met for dinner a few nights later, and the sparks seemed to fly. Soon they were spending most of their time together. Kaly listened to Bret describe his recent misfortunes. She felt the pain and confusion that Bret experienced and sought to lighten his load. Her heart opened to him. She knew he was vulnerable and that he needed to be loved and understood. Kaly sent Bret healing waves of love and understanding. Bret willingly soaked up the love and guidance she offered him. Kaly is an emotional intuitive, and her natural gift of empathy came into full bloom with Bret. She felt his feelings, comforted him when he needed it and, without being told, provided him what he needed to heal.

Kaly came to see me one hot summer day confused about why her relationship with Bret was not progressing. She felt a strong connection with him, and she believed that Bret felt it too. Despite this he had recently expressed a desire for a break in the relationship, and she didn't understand why. She knew that he was the one for her. She told me that she felt more love for him and understood him better than she had any previous boyfriend. Bret told her he loved her, but he had a nagging feeling that something was missing in the relationship.

Bret was wounded, and this triggered a depth of love and compassion in Kaly that she had not before experienced. Her intuition was also overly focused on Bret's process for healing. She offered him unconditional love and support, and because of that she ignored her intuitive warning system's signals to her of his lack of interest.

In intimate relationships, it is necessary that there be an equal energetic give and take. When you exert effort to heal and take care of another and in the process lose your center, you can create an imbalance that hinders the free flow of energy. Love is the ability to express and share of yourself from a place of inner empowerment. It requires that you receive as well as give. In order for a relationship to stay in balance, you must be as solidly connected to your own emotions and needs as you are to the other person's. Absolute love flows from an inner state of well-being.

The Temptation to Control Outcomes

Using intuitive information to control relationship outcomes is another common temptation.

David

David, a talented telecommunications engineer, called me from Italy. He had never worked with a psychic before, and I could tell he was skeptical. He had contacted me at the urging of his cousin, who was also a client. I knew that whatever his concern, it was important to him. I soon learned that he was seeking advice about his relationship with Jade, his girlfriend of a year and a half.

I knew when I looked into David's relationship with Jade that it would not last long. I could feel his hope and desire for a future with this woman, but I did not see it. While he was doing everything that he could think of to win her love, her energy spoke of lack of interest in him. I felt as if she would soon break up with him, and when I gently told him so he did not seem surprised. David then began to ask me questions about how to keep Jade from ending the relationship. He wanted to know if she would stay with him if he helped her to pay her bills. He asked me about her health and whether she needed to take vitamins or eat healthier. He thought that maybe this is why she lacked interest and enthusiasm. He asked about his home and possibly moving; he thought that perhaps a new home would appeal to her. The more questions David asked, the more intense and desperate he seemed to become. He wanted the love of this woman and he did not feel complete without her. He intuitively knew her fears and her hopes, and he devised ways to control her behavior. He was telepathically connecting to Jade in an attempt to know her thoughts and try to change her mind. He wanted energetic control over her, and he turned to a psychic to manage his anxiety and stress.

Using intuitive awareness to control others does not work. The better use of David's intuitive awareness would have been for him to focus on guidance that would help him to address his fears and his need to dominate others. Intuitive insight could also have provided him with the kind of guidance that would help him heal and release any inner obstacles, beliefs, or emotional wounds that might be preventing him from being in the kind of relationship that he so much desired.

The soul-mate relationship that David sought was not very far from him. I saw a loving, petite woman in his future. He needed to let go of Jade and transform his fears in order to attract this woman into his life.

It is not unusual to believe that a certain person can make you happy and that if you can just figure out how, you can make a relationship work. But the wisdom of love does not operate through our attempts at control and manipulation.

Absolute love operates in supply and abundance. There is an unlimited and boundless supply of love opportunities available to you. Intuitive awareness can lead to fulfilling and satisfying relationships, but you may have to release what you want it to look like.

The Problem of Potential

Another intuitive pitfall is the illusionary nature of potential. Intuitive awareness provides the gift of being able to see deeply into the soul of another. This can reveal another's rich potential and beauty. Where the material eyes see the outside appearance of another, intuitive vision perceives what lies deep within. A person may have a life full of difficulties and problems and have a cranky disposition, but you see beyond that. You may think that with enough love, understanding, and inspiration you can mend her broken wings and help her to soar. Unfortunately, awareness of another's potential does not mean that you have the power to change him or her. Neither does your awareness always motivate another to take action.

Everyone, regardless of intuitive type, will occasionally allow their intuitive impressions of others' potential capabilities to override their own practical judgment. The power of absolute love is so persuasive that we who are intuitively attuned to this intense vibration often forget that while we can often see the positive attributes of another, it is up to the individual to actualize their own potential. Unless they do, all the good that you may intuit about another will not manifest.

One of the most difficult lessons that I have had to learn in my relationships is that love can overcome all adversity, heal, and bring wholeness and well-being to any individual or relationship—but only when it is personally embraced. You and I cannot give that love to anyone. That choice belongs to the individual, and no matter how much we may want another to heal and change, it is their choice as to when and how.

Take Care of Yourself

Highly intuitive people can focus more on their concern for others than on their concern for their own well-being. People who are intuitively attuned often disregard the amount of energy, time, and responsibility that being in a relationship with another will have on them.

In the spiritual realms, all creative possibilities can be instantly realized. There is no time and space and no restraints on your inspired capabilities. In the physical and material realms, things take longer because you are working through time, space, and the collective consciousness. So, taking care of yourself and the precious gift of intuitive sensitivity has to be a priority. You cannot be a help to anyone else if you yourself are overwhelmed and stressed.

It is important to use your intuitive ability to tune in to the impact that another person will have on you. You are responsible for your choices and actions. It is not selfish or unloving to take care of yourself, even if it means you have to end or limit certain relationships.

At our core essence we are all beings of love; however, our human personality is not always easy to get along with. Even if you know another as divine spirit, their human personality may have a negative impact of you. Accepting others as they are, without negative judgment and criticism, is a lesson that we all must learn.

You do not have to get along, see eye to eye, and share conversation and dinner with everyone. Not everyone will like you and some will even misunderstand and judge you. This can be a source of pain, but it can also free you. Be you, and let others be who they are.

Stay Centered, Stay Loving
This exercise will help you become aware of what it feels like to stay centered in love while in a difficult or confusing relationship. Once your intuition has been activated, it is important to be conscious of the flow of energy between you and others. Otherwise, it becomes quite easy to slip into unhealthy and unproductive patterns of intuitive interaction.

- Find a relaxed position, and close your eyes. Take a long, deep breath, and as you exhale, release any stress and any tension you may be feeling. Take a few more breaths, inhaling deeply and calmly and then exhaling long and relaxed.

- Imagine a triangle. Within the triangle see an image of yourself. Picture yourself as clearly as possible.

- Ask for the presence of absolute love to enter this triangle with you. Imagine love seeping in and enveloping you with warm nurturing and a sense of well-being.

- Become comfortable with this love. Allow it to enter your heart. Love can sometimes feel unfamiliar, so we do not always let it in. Open your heart and let love energize and revitalize you.

- Ask for the presence of a particular person with whom you are in relationship to enter this triangle with you.

- When you feel as if this person has entered the triangle with you, ask your inner guidance the following questions:

    1. How does it feel to be in this person's presence?
    2. Is my sense of well-being dependent on another's actions or feelings toward me?
    3. What do I need to do to take care of myself in this relationship?
    4. What am I learning in my relationship with____?
    5 Open your heart and give your feelings and thoughts expression. Accept without judgment whatever surfaces.

- Pay attention to any feelings, impressions, and sensations that emerge. Tune in to bodily feelings, such as tension or stress, or openness and feelings of calm serenity. Use the technique of creating images from the energy that you receive. Feel, listen, and ask for guidance. Interpret your impressions.

- Ask for love to heal and restore inner balance and harmony.

- Breathe and remain in open and loving receptivity for as long as possible.

- When you feel as if you are finished, open your eyes and write down the impressions, advice, and guidance that you received. Commit to actions that reinforce self-love and care.

Finding the balance between loving yourself and loving another, the equal give and take of a relationship, is never easy. Remember, love is energy. Being able to intuitively tune in to the flow of love energy between you and another will help you to stay centered, while at the same time giving to that person in healthy ways.

It is only when your relationships have healthy and balanced boundaries that you are free to love. Being intuitive is no excuse for becoming enmeshed in others' emotions, thoughts, issues, and behavior.

Use your intuition wisely and set yourself free to love!

11

HOW TO READ OTHERS EFFECTIVELY

∿∿∿∿∿∿∿∿∿∿∿∿∿∿∿∿∿∿∿∿∿∿∿∿∿∿∿∿

We all want to know more about the people who pique our interest and occupy our heart and mind. Haven't we all at some point been left wondering about the intent, emotions, and thoughts of those we are attracted to and those we love? Even in long-term relationships, the person we have spent many years with can still in some ways be a mystery. We are complex creatures, always capable of surprising those we love.

Stumbling Blocks to Reading Others

Your intuition can provide you with another way to know those you are in relationship with, and insight into those whom you might just be curious about. There are, however, a few things to consider. The more emotionally involved you are with the person you are tuning in to, the more difficult it can be for your perceptions to be impartial and objective. When you desire a certain outcome, your intuition will be less clear and accurate. Expectations can act like the static on the telephone line. Your intuitive ability is still at work, but the receptiveness is compromised.

Excessive influence by the ego can sabotage your intuitive attempts. Remember the ego is that part of us that feels separate from love. It feels as if it must strategize and control others and the environment to get what it wants. The ego will try to motivate you through fear, thoughts, and feelings—don't let it. When you feel love as stress, move your awareness within; calm yourself with deep, cleansing breaths; and open the heart. When your heart is open with acceptance and flowing with the current of absolute love, your intuitive receptivity will be more focused and lucid.

Release Expectations

The key to using your intuition to know and understand another better is to develop a detached, nonjudgmental, and accepting state of heart and mind. It is important to acknowledge the feelings, beliefs, and expectations that you have surrounding a particular person or relationship, then be willing to let them go. This does not mean that you no longer care or that what you most want will not happen. Expectations are a form of control. It keeps our energy from freely flowing into higher levels of awareness and intuitive receptivity. Releasing conscious control is a bold step that allows the truth to be revealed. It will allow you to come into an open and receptive state that is essential for increasing intuitive awareness. Letting go empowers you to receive intuitive information and guidance with clarity.

Setting the Stage

The following exercise can be used before you tune in to the energy of others. It can also be used when you find yourself trying to control another or becoming anxious about the outcome of a relationship.

Releasing and Receiving

- Choose a person with whom you have a relationship or someone whom you would like to be in a relationship with. Imagine your relationship with the person a month, six months, a year, and five years into the future. Write down your expectations. How would you like the relationship to be, what are your thoughts and feelings about the relationship in the future?

- Now, close your eyes and begin to breathe in cleansing breaths, relaxing and breathing out any stress and tension. Keep breathing in and releasing, becoming more and more relaxed with each breath.

- Bring into your awareness your expectations. Imagine that these expectations have energy, and this energy is lodged somewhere in your body in the form of stress or tension. Quite often it is in the head, neck, shoulders, heart, or stomach area.

- As you locate areas of stress, imagine that you can release and let go of this energy simply by drawing your awareness to it and breathing into it. The intention to release is often all that you'll need.

- As you release the expectations, imagine that the space that they have occupied within your body is now filled with love and openness. Imagine clear space and awareness filling these areas.

- Breathe and feel the open presence filling you. You are light, unencumbered and free. You release those you love and care about into this light and expansive openness, allowing them to be themselves. You give the gift of love and freedom to yourself and all others.

This exercise can be practiced over and over, and it can be effective in a multitude of situations. It brings with it feelings of inner peace and serenity. As you continue to clear yourself and release your expectations of others, you will begin to maintain an open and receptive state, which is crucial for accurate intuitive perception.

Insight into Another

The following exercise will empower you to see more deeply into another. It is important to go into this exercise with curiosity and objectivity.

In this exercise you will use the skill of psychometry. As I've mentioned, psychometry is the ability to receive intuitive impressions from holding a personal object or a picture of another person. Pictures and personal objects, like a piece of often-worn jewelry, hold the energetic imprint of an individual. The premise of psychometry is that our intuitive sensors will tune in to another's vibration from the object or picture and interpret what is received.

Physical intuitives tend to receive information naturally, through objects and pictures, but all of the types with a few adjustments can effectively use psychometry. For the emotional intuitive it is important to pay attention to whatever emotions or feelings surface, and then with the technique previously outlined, transfer these emotions into an image. The mental intuitive may connect telepathically with the person they are "reading" and intuit their thoughts, while the spiritual intuitive may easily see visions, imagery, and colors. They just need to trust and record their perceptions.

Visualize a House

This visualization exercise helps you more fully tune in to another's energy field. If you do not have a photograph or the person's personal object, write down his or her name and birthday. Enter into this meditative visualization with the intent of learning more about the person without judgment and expectation.

In this exercise the metaphor of a house is used to represent the other person's energy. Use your imagination; even if you feel as if you are making it all up, go with it. Remember that if your visualization makes good sense to your logical mind, then your intuition is not fully engaged.

Intuitive energy is often invoked through creativity. In this exercise you will draw and sketch; however, you don't have to be an artist to do well. It is not the quality of the drawing that is important. Rather, it is the stimulation of active, creative work that allows your intuitive knowing to surface. Find a piece of plain white paper and an assortment of different colored pens, pencils, or markers for this exercise.

Approach this exercise with a sense of playfulness and imagination; it will enhance your intuitive ability. Don't try to figure out or make sense of what you receive. Just observe the energy, without projecting your own desires. Be open, and invite what is; be like a reporter, just collecting the facts.

Now, sit in a comfortable position and hold the person's object or photograph in your hands. You may find that you don't even need to look at the picture. Pictures, like personal objects, hold an energetic imprint. You can connect with the person's vibration simply by holding the photo. If you do want to look at the photo, take a few moments to do so before you continue.

- Close your eyes and take a long, deep breath, and send the energy of the breath to any part of your body that is sore or tense or tight. Exhale the tension and stress. Take another breath and a long, deep, relaxing exhale. This time, breathing in from the top of your head, send the breath through your body, relaxing and exhaling. As you breathe in, you can imagine that the breath descending down through the top of your head as relaxing white light. Send this white light through your body.

- As you continue the natural rhythm of this calming breathing, imagine you are in a place in nature where you feel safe and relaxed. There may be a gentle breeze blowing through the trees, and vegetation and flowers of all shapes and colors gracing the landscape. You can feel the sun shine down on you, helping you to feel even more relaxed. This warm sunlight represents all that you desire in your life, such as abundance, connection, love, and joy. You might hear water flowing from a stream or waterfall in the background or the sound of birds calling to one another. Whatever sounds or sensations that you experience help you to become more and more relaxed.

- Notice a path leading into a grove of trees. Begin to walk this dirt-and-stone-lined path, making your way through the trees and into a clearing. The path winds down a short incline, and in the distance you see a house. This is the house of the person whose object or picture you hold.

- Explore the house; you are welcome here. Walk to the front of the house. As you get closer, notice the front of the house. What color is it? Is it a small house, a large and rambling house, more than one story, quaint, or newly built? Is the front yard landscaped or in a natural state? Is there a front porch? Notice the front door; do you get a sense of its color or material?

- Open your eyes and sketch the front of the house. As you draw, you might want to add certain features to the house that you did not see in your visualization. Go ahead and do it.

- Close your eyes and imagine that you are now entering the house through the front door. Notice that you are now in the living room. Take your time and notice everything you can about the living room. Is it well furnished and neat, or is it in disarray or simply well lived in? Are there curtains on the windows, or does light stream in? What color are the walls? Are the furnishings modern, contemporary, or eclectic? Are there antiques or other interesting objects?

- Open your eyes and draw the living room in detail. Include all the colors and objects that you see.

- Close your eyes and pay attention to any sensations, feelings, or thoughts that you experience in this house. Are you comfortable or uneasy? Do you feel as if you are intruding, or do you feel welcome?

- Imagine that you are now entering the kitchen; it is in the back of the house. Is it well used, equipped with many cooking utensils, or is it small and sparse and looks barely used? Is there a kitchen table? How big is it? What color is the kitchen? Is there a clock? What time is it? How does it feel to be in the kitchen?

- When you feel as if you have explored the kitchen, open your eyes and make a drawing of it. Again, as you draw you can add anything else that comes to mind.

- Close your eyes, leave the kitchen, and look for the stairs. Go up the stairs and imagine what the upper level is like. Are there bedrooms, bathrooms, or other finished spaces? If there is a bedroom, go in and observe it. What color is it? How big is the bed? Is it neatly made or is it unmade? Is the room dark or light? Are there windows, curtains, or open light? Maybe this level is an unfinished attic, empty or full of boxes and other things? Is it dark, light, well used, or rarely used?

- When you have explored the upstairs, open your eyes and sketch what you observed.

- Close your eyes and go downstairs and look around. Maybe you notice new things. Are there closets? If so, open one and see what is inside. Are there shelves or bookcases, perhaps a fireplace? Does it feel comfortable to be in this house? Notice anything that you can about the house, especially your feelings and sense of it. Does it feel familiar? Does it bring up any memories or unpleasant thoughts? How does it feel to be in this person's house? Can you imagine living here or staying for a visit? Would you be comfortable here?

- Open your eyes and draw anything else that you observe in the house. If feelings, memories, or thoughts surface, write them down.

- When you are ready, close your eyes, find the back door, and go through it to the backyard. Notice whatever you can about its condition. Is it well kept with a garden or flowers, a playground? Is it in a natural state with trees, bushes, and perhaps a pond or stream? Take one last scan of this house, paying special attention to any thoughts that surface, feelings, or emotions, and any sensations that you feel in your body. Do not dismiss anything as unimportant.

- Open your eyes and draw the backyard of the house and any other information, impressions, or observations that have come to you.
- Close your eyes and notice that there is a path leading away from the house. Take this path, and you will find that it leads you back to the place you started. In your special place in nature, whenever you want to do this exercise you can return here.
- Open your eyes when you are ready and draw or write down any additional thoughts, feelings, or observations.

Increasing Your Symbolic Vocabulary

It is important to trust and build a personal inner symbolic foundation on which to interpret the images you receive during intuitive exercises. It is always best to defer to your own inner sense of what is right for you. However, the following are interpretations of common metaphors and symbols. Use what feels right to you. Trust your ability to know what these, and other, symbols, metaphors, and images signify to you.

Houses

Houses represent individual energy. Different parts of the house represent aspects of the personality, character, and tendencies. The front of the house represents the personality-self that an individual presents to the world. A front lawn that is well tended or lined with trimmed bushes, or an orderly stone path, represents a person who is concerned with his or her appearance, orderly, and organized. Such a person may care very much about how others view him or her. Flowers and greenery are positive symbols of affection and love. A home with a big porch suggests friendliness and openness. A brick or stone house is a metaphor for strength—this might be physical, mental, or emotional. Brick and stone might also indicate a grounded, stable personality. If the house is small without many windows, it may suggest a person who is more private and contained.

The interior of the house reveals more of the person's personality. Antique or older furniture represents a person who is connected to his or her past. If the furniture or general condition of the house is poor, the person may have work to do on past issues and wounds. If you feel comfortable in the house, then the person may be open and ready to welcome someone into their lives. If there is a fireplace or large hearth, the person is heart centered. A fire in the fireplace may indicate generosity and passion. Many windows and sunlight indicates he or she is open to possibilities and is warm and clear minded.

If you feel uncomfortable or as if you are intruding in the house, it could mean that the person may not be open or ready to bring another person into his or her life. A lot of things, especially boxes, cluttered shelves, and closets can indicate someone with unfinished business. This could take the form of issues, secrets, unresolved concerns, or emotions.

Rooms

The kitchen represents a person's ability to nurture. A small, rarely used kitchen expresses someone who may not be a natural nurturer. A large, well-used kitchen may be someone who enjoys caring and giving to others.

The upper level of a house represents a person's higher consciousness or spirituality. A missing, dark, or unfinished upper level may indicate an undeveloped higher awareness. A light, airy, open upper level indicates someone who is in touch with his or her spiritual energy or is clairvoyant or open minded.

The bedroom usually indicates sexual nature. A large bedroom or big comfortable bed is someone who is at ease with his or her sexuality. Again, it is important to pay attention to how you feel or the thoughts that surface while you are in the bedroom. Feeling relaxed in the bedroom may indicate affection and sexual attraction, while feeling ill at ease may show sexual incompatibility.

The backyard of a house shows a person's past or what the person has put behind them. A garden or flowers show resolution and order. A playground indicates a playful or childish nature, or it could indicate a desire for children. Water anywhere in or around the house shows the emotional or spiritual nature of the person. A small, murky pond illustrates cloudy or stagnant emotions. A river, stream, fountain, or ocean view is a positive symbol of emotional energy and vital life-force energy.

Colors

The colors in the house also have significance. Red represents energy, life force, passion, and sexuality. It may also be a signal to stop. Pink is the energy of love, warmth, and acceptance. Orange represents creativity, positive energy, and fun. Yellow is symbolic of sunshine, playful feelings, and youthfulness. Yellow can also represent fear and insecurity. Green represents health, healing, and perhaps wealth and money. Blue can signify calmness, loyalty, strength, and wisdom. It can also point to depression and sad feelings. Purple or indigo can represent richness, magic, and power. It is often a color of spiritual attainment and clairvoyance. White illustrates what is pure, fresh, clean, and good. It can stand for another's connection with divine, life-giving energy. Brown can be a color for a down-to-earth, grounded person, but it might also suggest someone is stuck in the past. Black can represent negativity and evil, and might be a warning. Black can also mean material power and a well-grounded, secure personality. The shades and overall mood you feel with color is also important. Do the colors feel vibrant or dark and depressing?

The Overall Message

It is particularly important to pay attention to the feelings, emotions, thoughts, and memories that surface while you are in the house. If you feel as if you have been in this house before, or a very similar one, then ask yourself if this atmosphere is right for you; does it appeal to you or is it uninteresting and lacking? Examine any thoughts or memories that you had during the exercise. If there are thoughts or memories of a past relationship or experience you have been through, ask yourself if this was a positive time for you, did you feel loved?

Be honest with your impressions, even if you have no concrete evidence that would verify or justify what your intuition is telling you. Self-trust might be the most difficult part of the exercise.

Variations on House Visualization

Get an overall sense of the house. If you feel as if there is no cohesive message or you are still confused as to how to interpret your impressions, write a story about the house based on impressions you did have.

One variation of this exercise for people who feel more comfortable writing is to hold the person's object or look at the picture and write nonstop about his or her house. Try to keep in the flow of uninterrupted writing. This is called automatic writing, and it can reveal surprising results.

Another approach is to imagine your own house. Not the house you live in now or have lived in, but a house that is symbolic of who you are. After you have done this, invite your person into your house and observe what happens. Are they willing to come in? Do you really want her in your home? Is it comfortable or awkward to have him walk through your house? Again be as honest about your observations.

It is interesting that some people actually intuit the physical home of the person they are tuning in to. Even if you suspect that you are seeing a real house, you can still gain valuable information. You can still get a sense of how it feels to be in another's space and energy.

The more you use this exercise, the more it will strengthen your ability to tune in to energy, create images and symbols, and interpret the images into valuable information. This is the foundation of successful intuitive ability.

12

TUNE IN TO YOU
AND TRANSFORM
YOUR RELATIONSHIPS

U se your intuition for deeper self-understanding. We all want to experience loving and satisfying relationships. It seems simple, yet the authentic feelings of love often elude us. Despite our best efforts, we are sometimes unable to sustain positive intimacy with others, and we do not know why.

Love has a unique alchemy that, like water in a river or an ocean or pond, is shaped by its environment. Relationships reveal our capacity for kindness, forgiveness, and compassion, as well as our fears and insecurities. The love you experience in relationships is shaped by who you are. It is a direct reflection of your innermost thoughts, beliefs, past experiences, and ability to love yourself. The path to creating more happiness, joy, and intimacy in your relationships begins by looking within.

Self-awareness is not always as straightforward as we would like it to be. We are, for the most part, unaware of the powerful energies that shape our lives. Deliberate intuition focused in the area of self-awareness can bring to light hidden aspects of your nature that may be preventing you from experiencing loving and satisfying relationships. Once you become aware of what might be hindering the full expression of love in your life, you can heal and move forward. Transforming your relationships begins with transforming yourself. True, lasting change originates at the depths of your being.

Understanding the Unconscious

To use intuition for self-growth and healing, you will need to understand the unconscious. The unconscious, or subconscious, is that part of you of which you are unaware. The conscious and unconscious are not always in sync with one another. As an example, let's say you long for a loving, intimate relationship. If, however, your unconscious mind harbors the belief that you are not worthy of love, or relationships never work out for you, your efforts to create intimacy with others will be sabotaged.

Your unconscious holds a perfect record of everything that you have ever experienced. Every thought, emotion, even every word that you have spoken and action taken, is perfectly recorded within your inner mind. The unconscious does not judge or choose what it responds to. It simply creates your reality based on what it energetically holds. When emotional wounds, fears, or limiting beliefs remain in the unconscious, you attract people who have similar energy. The unconscious can interfere with your best efforts to create loving relationships. Until you release the unhealed hurts and pain, you continue to draw similar wounds and issues to yourself. These patterns of relationships, left unhealed, can last an entire lifetime. Many of our most difficult relationships are the result of patterns of behavior and beliefs to which we are unconsciously responding. Until you are conscious of what needs healing, you will continue to leave a negative relationship or situation only to find yourself getting into another one.

Intuitive awareness can help you gain conscious access to your energetic memory. It can send powerful rays of absolute love and healing energy into the cloudy past.

The Next Step

You have developed the basics for using your natural intuition in relationships. They are:

1. Create a question
2. Perceive the energy surrounding the question
3. Create images, symbols, and metaphors that represent this energy
4. Interpret your impressions through a combination of logic and intuition

We will now add to your intuitive repertoire the practice of symbolic vision.

Symbolic vision is the ability to intuit meaning and guidance by observing what occurs in our everyday lives. It is the ability to perceive the connection between your deeper beliefs and emotional patterns and the circumstances and conditions that you are experiencing in your life. It means that you see beyond appearances and right into the soulful gut of a situation. When you view what is happening in a relationship as symbolic of an unconscious need for love and healing, you can do the necessary work to heal and move forward. Intuitive awareness can shine a little light into that darkness.

Developing Symbolic Vision

Symbolic vision is a bit like dream interpretation. In a dream, we look at the different parts, characters, and objects as having a deeper meaning or message—flowers, for instance, can represent growth and hope, and a turbulent ocean can signify chaotic emotions. You can apply this same principle to your life.

Sarah

My client Sarah had repeated car accidents that damaged the front bumper of her car. She wondered what this might mean; was there a message for her in these constant accidents?

At the time she was separated from her husband and in the process of divorcing. She was fearful of moving forward in life, especially financially. She was attempting to start three businesses at the same time. She couldn't decide which she wanted most, so she tried to do all three. This was wearing on her emotionally, physically, spiritually, and mentally. Sarah came to the awareness that the accidents may be symbolic of her need to slow down and take better care of herself. She was pushing herself beyond her limits and criticizing her own efforts. The dented front bumper illustrated to her how she was treating herself. Cars can be symbolic of how we move through life, and she realized that she was damaging and sabotaging her attempts to move forward.

Symbolic vision encourages intuitive development in that it trains the thinking mind to interpret reality differently, more energetically than materially. When you interpret the circumstances of your life in this way, you are no longer a victim of life's ups and downs; rather, you are empowered to view life events as opportunities for growth. Energy is not limited to time, space, or form—and symbolic vision shows you that neither are you limited.

Although it can sometimes be difficult to discern the lesson, the people with whom we have relationships are often the best teachers. You may repeat the same challenging relationship lessons over and over again, at a loss as to how to change the pattern. Even when you leave a difficult relationship, it is not uncommon to attract the same emotional circumstances with the next person. The way out of this endless cycle of repeating limiting patterns is to go deep within. You can free yourself to create new ways of relating when you dive into and heal limiting beliefs and negative patterns.

The following exercise is based on the idea that what happens in your daily life is a message from a deep and wise part of yourself. This exercise can help you understand the significance of your relationship challenges. In it, the negative aspects of a relationship are understood to be indicators of hidden emotional wounds and limiting beliefs that need to be healed.

Preparation
This visualization exercise incorporates the use of descriptive imagery. It is best if you make an audio recording and then close your eyes, relax, and proceed. Although I use imagery, it may be that you do not actually see or visually imagine what

I suggest. That is fine. Many people will just know or feel the suggestions.

The intuitive impressions you receive may come in a variety of ways. You may see random or symbolic images, or you may experience a persistent thought or feeling. You might hear the verse of a song, or feel enveloped by a gentle warmth and loving presence. Just allow what feels right for you to surface and go with it.

You may feel as if you do not receive much intuitive information. If so, pay attention over the next few days to your dreams, daydreams, and episodes of synchronicity. Energy information can surface when we least expect it, even days or weeks later.

Ask Your Question

Begin by identifying a relationship pattern that you would like to change. Focus on an area of confusion or unhappiness. This might be an issue that you are experiencing in a current relationship or it might be an unresolved past issue. Perhaps you feel ignored or treated less lovingly than you would like. You may still wonder why a past partner did not return the kind of love you felt for him or her.

Pay attention to whatever feelings emerge as you write. Write these down, too, and do not judge what you feel; be as honest and forthright as possible. Now imagine that these circumstances and feelings have nothing to do with the other person. What you are experiencing is a reflection of the part of you that needs your attention.

- Once you have written down the question, find a relaxing position and close your eyes. Take a deep, long breath and exhale any stress or tension. You may have strong emotional feelings after having written down your concerns; this is to be expected. Do not try to push those feelings away, allow them to surface. Breathe into them, and feel them.

- Take a few more breaths, breathing in deeply and calmly and then exhaling long, relaxed breaths. As you continue breathing, allow any thoughts to surface. Take note of them and breathe them out as you exhale; continue with this relaxed breathing.

- Now, visualize a triangle and in the center of this triangle imagine that there a door. Even if you do not clearly see the door, do your best to create it in your imagination.

- Imagine that within the doorway is an aspect of you that wants your attention. This is an aspect that needs healing.

- Open the door and look inside. Become aware of the *you* that greets you there. Allow an image to emerge that represents this part of you. It may look like you, like a child you, like an older you, like a sad or frustrated you, or it may not look anything like you at all. The image may be the opposite sex or a different race, but it *is* the part of you that needs your love.

- If necessary, use your imagination and create an image that feels right to you. Adopt a curious observing attitude toward this part of you. Be open and receive any impressions, feelings, or thoughts this image can communicate to you.

- Now imagine that you, as you are in present time, enter the triangle. Imagine that the present-time you leads the unhealed you through the doorway. Imagine that as you do, the space surrounding the two of you is filled with brilliant light. This light feels warm and comforting. Take a few moments to breathe this healing love into your heart. You may feel, see, or sense the presence of light or of your angels supporting this process.

- You can communicate with the unhealed you and ask what it most needs from you. Take a few minutes to listen quietly and receive anything that surfaces.

  This information may be a thought, a feeling, a memory, a spontaneous welling-up of emotion, or a simple, deep sense of knowing. What does your unhealed aspect need in order to heal?

- Commit to taking any action that will empower and help this aspect of you to feel loved and accepted. Listen to your fears, and resolve to take loving care of yourself. As you do this, imagine the brilliant light of absolute love purifying and healing any stress, negativity, fear, or pain. Imagine that this now-healed part of you merges into your heart.

- When you feel as if you have received all that you can at this time, take a few deep breaths and imagine you are absorbing all that you need to know, feel, and experience. When you are ready, open your eyes and immediately write down your impressions. Write down any feelings in your body, any thoughts, or any visual images. Do not try and figure it all out yet, just write it down.

What you experience in this exercise may not make much sense at first. You do not have to figure it all out. The intuitive unfolding process often takes some time. Know that when you are ready, you will understand what you need to know. Continue this exercise as often as you need to. Healing is an unfolding process that has its own rhythm and wisdom. Trust that there are powerful forces for healing that are assisting you and caring for you.

Healing Is a Loving Act

As you shift your attitudes and heal the unsatisfying and unfulfilling patterns within, your relationships naturally transform. The most loving act you can do for others is to heal yourself, as self-healing sets in motion an energetic pattern that motivates others to heal. Even if those in your relationships do not acknowledge the changes that you have made, the presence of love and healing still influences them.

Theresa
My client Theresa told me about her experience with this exercise. When I first met Theresa, she was lonely and confused. She had not been in an intimate relationship for many years. In her heart she longed for the closeness of a partner, but she was running out of hope that she would find one. She tried to resign herself to being alone, but the thought of it made her sad.

Theresa said she'd never felt truly loved by a man. She dated some in her youth and was once engaged to man when she was in her mid-twenties, but they had agreed to break the engagement because they realized they were more friends than loving partners.

Theresa was eager to develop her intuitive skills, so she enrolled in a class I was teaching. She hoped she could gain insight into her relationships. Over the years Theresa had met men through dating and matchmaking services, through friends, and through chance encounters. She told me that when she met a potential partner it always seemed as if either she wasn't attracted to him, or he to her. Attraction never seemed to be mutual, and Theresa seemed to despair of ever finding someone.

Theresa began this exercise by contemplating the common thread that ran through her relationships and her current feelings. She felt hopeless and unlovable. She realized that as far back as childhood she'd had these same feelings. She realized that it began with her father, who sat every evening in front of the television, drinking. He was emotionally distant and didn't seem to notice her.

Theresa went into the meditation with mixed feelings and on the verge of tears. She did her best to visualize a large white door. When she imagined herself opening the door, she felt the part of herself that was scared and disappointed. This part did not feel as if it deserved love. As she listened and opened herself to this energy, an image of a lost and lonely little girl began to form. This aspect of her felt at fault that people did not love her. If she were prettier or smarter, then she believed they would love her. She simply did not feel good enough for love.

Theresa coaxed this little-girl part of her out of the doorway. She took the little girl's hand and asked her what she needed in order to heal and feel more lovable. The little girl told her that she needed to be listened to and cared for. This little Theresa asked her to love her as much as she loved her poodles. (Theresa had three poodles that she adores, and her love and care for them knew no boundaries.)

Theresa assured the little girl that she would take care of herself better. She would listen to her feelings and act in loving and compassionate ways toward herself. As she sent the little girl this message, she could feel a stronger, more loving connection to her. Theresa opened her heart and let the little girl in.

Integration

Awareness is the first step to transforming the unconscious beliefs and emotional patterns that keep you locked into relationship behaviors that no longer serve your highest good. Once you recognize the influences that have been motivating your choices, you are able to heal and move in a different direction. This is authentic and lasting transformation. With ease you are now able to manifest the conditions and circumstances that reflect your inner clarity. Releasing the stuffed-away pain and negative beliefs and patterns allows for the flow of positive and loving energy to reshape your life.

The next step to reinforce transformation is to integrate your renewed inner self-awareness into your outer life. You can do this by committing to positive and affirming action that expresses your highest good.

Theresa knew she needed to spend time each day listening to her long-silenced inner voice. She needed to commit to behaviors that fortified her loving, authentic self. She had not been compassionate or loving toward herself, and because of this she attracted the same behavior from others. How we love ourselves is how others will love us.

Theresa made a list of activities that interested her but she never had the time or energy for. She had long ago given up her childhood pleasure of dance, so she enrolled in a hip-hop dance class at the local arts council. She began to read more about the angelic realm and meditated daily with the hope of establishing a stronger connection to her angels. Theresa bought another dog and named him after her first crush, Kyle, who had asked her out on her first date. Her heart opened with young love many years ago when dating Kyle, and she wanted to rekindle those feelings of innocence. She was determined to give herself the attention she longed for from a partner, and Kyle would be her reminder to do just that.

The Cycle of Healing

You can use symbolic vision in almost every aspect of your life. It can provide additional information on any condition or situation.

Healing yourself allows your relationships to come into greater harmony. You will attract those who reflect your inner well-being, and the influence of positive energy will steer your current relationships toward healing and wholeness.

13

MOVE OUT OF RELATIONSHIP STAGNATION AND INTO JOY

Invite absolute love into your life and experience its power to renew and revitalize your relationships. To experience the kind of love that we all desire, it is necessary that our energy connections with others be centered in our most pure love.

Open and honest verbal communication is a necessary ingredient for a successful relationship. Energetic communication is just as important. You are constantly and unceasingly emitting through your energy field the energy vibration of your thoughts, intent, emotions, beliefs, and the truth of who you are. What and how you energetically relate to another dictates what you will experience in the relationship.

Unfortunately, we often and unknowingly bond with others through our common limitations and misery or through superficial personality traits. Feeling an instantaneous, intuitive connection to someone does not always indicate that you will have a positive and meaningful relationship with him or her. It may be that the attraction is based on similar negative thought or emotional patterns. The adrenaline chemical-energetic rush of falling in love is the meeting of two well-matched energy fields. But the match may not necessarily be a positive and unconditionally loving one.

When you connect with another through less-evolved aspects of yourself, you run the risk of continuing the unhealed and superficial patterns. Eventually what first felt like familiarity and shared experiences will begin to feel like lack and dissatisfaction.

Filling in the Missing Pieces

Whether we realize it or not, we sometimes enter into relationships to make up for our deficits and to fulfill our needs. For instance, if you feel as if you are not able to earn a high salary, you may be attracted to someone who does. If you feel shy or introverted, you may want a partner who is socially confident and entertaining. Some people who have had difficult childhoods will be attracted to a partner who they feel can make up for their past lack of love and affection.

We also connect with others through our strengths. If you feel an abundance of love, you may attempt to compensate for another's feelings of lack and overwhelm her with your love. You may feel a need to rescue other people who feel victimized by life's circumstances. Or, you may desire to heal and uplift others and enter into relationships with the good but misguided intention to change people.

When we mistake another as our source of wholeness or if we feel we can complete another, we not only remain imbalanced but we create imbalance within the relationship. One of the problems with the unconscious pattern of seeking balance in another is that it creates an energetic pattern of lack. If you continue to bond with others in this way, then you are depending on a source outside of yourself for a sense of well-being. You create unhealthy patterns within yourself and within your relationships when you halt the growth process to fulfill another's expectations, or expect that others will halt theirs for your benefit.

Creating Unhealthy Energy Connections
The area where I live is experiencing a severe drought. The rivers are drying up; many lakes and ponds already have. I see parched ground where a pond had been, and I feel sympathy for the small fish, frogs, and turtles whose environment has been eradicated. Not all things seem fair and balanced. Areas to the north and west are reporting record rainfall, little solace to the vulnerable and now homeless life forms that just last year were thriving. I fantasize that a huge pipe could be built that would connect these overflowing waterways to the north and west, which now flow into the sea, to the rivers here that have dwindled to streams.

Like the rain-starved land, some people live in a love drought. Perhaps their parents were love starved and had little love to give. Some people feel unworthy of love while others simply do not know how to recognize and receive love. The consciousness of the world we live in reinforces the scarcity of love. So, we search and look to one another to fill the void.

Like my fantasy pipeline, we connect to others to add what is missing. While this may seem to make perfect sense, in truth connections to others based on excess and deficit eventually lead to an energetic gridlock, which does not allow for growth and change.

The reality is that you become disempowered when you create connections in order to try and borrow another's energy to compensate for what you lack. Likewise, you will also become weary when you attempt to give to another to make up for his feelings of lack. There is a difference between being supportive, loving, and compassionate and subordinating another's growth process.

Love Is Evolution

The connections that you have established with others to compensate for your strengths and weaknesses may work for many years. Eventually, though, you will become restless and feel an inner urge to heal and grow. The universe flows in the direction of evolution, and its current is always pulling you forward. The stagnant connection that you have with another will at some point become unsatisfying and suffocating. This is a crucial time when some people choose to leave the relationship while others stay, and take up the challenge to change and evolve.

Shift from Relative Love to Absolute Love

To experience fulfilling, joy-filled relationships that celebrate the wholeness of each individual, your heart must break through the boundaries of personality-based love and instead love from the soul. The requirements for a healthy relationship—honesty, acceptance, forgiveness, compassion, and a putting aside of one's personal wants—move one into the deeper recesses of love. This kind of love, the love that creates mutually satisfying relationships, can only be found in the soul. The ego and the personality-self operate in getting, not in giving, and in fear instead of in love.

To love from the depths of the soul each partner must look within themselves. Where once you might have had high hopes of finding all the love you need in another, you must find it instead within you. This, I recognize, seems like quite a paradox, considering we usually seek out relationships to be loved. Yet when your happiness and well-being depend on another, you lose sight of you own inner source of love. Relationships collapse under the strain of overwhelming expectations, and you feel let down and disappointed. You can lovingly support your partner in their process, but you cannot walk the path for him or her.

Finding the Love Within

Absolute love is always with you and is your core essence. To come fully into its presence you need only draw within and listen to its ever-present voice. Your intuitive sensitivity can help you to detect and align yourself with the presence of absolute love. You may feel it as a flush of inner warmth and comfort and an openhearted ability to give and receive love. It is the unshakable inner assurance that, despite outward conditions, there is a plan and purpose for you in your relationships.

Absolute love in a relationship does not bind people together. Rather, it provides an inexhaustible source of wisdom, compassion, and forgiveness that each partner can draw upon to restore themselves and the relationship. Despite disappointments and failures, you will experience love in a new way when you invite absolute love to flow through you.

Kristine and Steven

I first met Kristine and her husband, Steven, at one of my workshops. They are a good example of a couple who traveled the path of healing both individually and together.

Kristine and Steven have been married for more than ten years. They met in college, when Kristine was a curious student who studied philosophy, the arts, and dance. Steven was a more serious student who graduated early with a degree in engineering. Kristine was initially attracted to Steven's handsome good looks and his sensible approach to life. She felt safe and cared for with him. For his part, Steven basked in the richness of Kristine's emotional warmth and love. She was affectionate and demonstrative and seemed to know the right things to say to lift his spirits and help him feel understood.

Steven grew up in a family where excelling in school and sports was expected, but it never mattered to Kristine if he was at the top of the class. She just loved him. Steven had never felt this kind of love before, and he proposed to Kristine soon after he started a high-paying job at a well-respected engineering firm. To Kristine it was heaven and all that she desired. She could pursue her painting and poetry, and she could continue on her spiritual path, knowing Steven would provide for her. Kristine and Steven lived in this balance of love, passion, and abundant finances for several years.

Eventually, Kristine began to feel emotionally empty. As the demands of his job increased, Steven came home from work later and was always preoccupied. She wanted to feel his strong arms holding her, but Steven was often too tired. He would collapse on the couch with little to say or give to her. Kristine looked to her friends for companionship and support. Steven could hear her on the phone late into the night with them, her voice light and full of laughter. He saw her interesting metaphysical books on the night table and he envied her curiosity. Steven would sneak a peek at them, but he didn't have the time or energy to devote to reading.

Frustration and resentment began to take root. Kristine wanted more affection and attention from Steven. Steven wanted Kristine to get a job and help take some of the financial pressure off of him. He wanted to have time away from work for his own self-exploration. Kristine felt Steven's growing emotional distance and longed for a devoted lover. She began to fantasize about being with other men.

Kristine's and Steven's patterns of relating and connecting to one another were beginning to become unsatisfying for both of them. They began to talk about divorce. In energetic language, they were stuck in a chakra holding pattern. Kristine's heart and spiritual energy reached out and connected to Steven early in the relationship. She sent a vibrant cord of love and spiritual energy to fill his emptiness. He soaked in this love and did not develop his capacity to express and give love in return. For his part, Steven was stuck in the pattern of sending material power and security to Kristine. She accepted this energy and did little to build up her confidence and experience in matters of work and finance. They were energetically dependent on one another.

Kristine, in her pursuit of the spiritual, did not develop herself in the world, while Steven's preoccupation with material matters stifled his spiritual and emotional development. They looked to one another to compensate for their lack of growth in these areas.

Eventually, though, this backfired. Kristine felt as if Steven was withholding love. She did not understand that he did not actually know how to feel and express the kind of love she now desired. Steven felt as if Kristine was lazy and self-centered. He did not understand that she had no idea how to have a job and earn money.

Kristine and Steven were stuck in the grip of relative love. Their way of relating to one another represents just one way that a relationship can become stagnant and locked in an unhealthy emotional-spiritual energy pattern. There are many others. To enjoy a loving and sustaining connection with another, it is necessary to break free from these stifling patterns.

Exercise

Here is an intuitive exercise to help you explore and heal the energetic connections you have established with another person. This is a good exercise to practice when you feel stuck in a relationship, especially when positive feelings are diminishing or the level of intimacy between you and another seems stagnant. This exercise can also be helpful if you cannot leave a relationship despite repeated attempts, or if a relationship has ended but you cannot seem to let go of it and move forward.

Shift from Relative Love to Absolute Love

This exercise requires paper, colored pencils, or markers. The creative process opens us to the natural flow of intuition. In this exercise you will draw and sketch. Don't worry if you are not an artist, just do your best. Don't criticize; give yourself the freedom to create and use your imagination!

- Begin by relaxing in a comfortable position. Think of a person with whom you have a current relationship or have had a past relationship. Close your eyes and take a few deep, cleansing breaths, imagining that you are inhaling white light from the top of your head. Let this breath descend through your entire body, relaxing you. As you exhale, imagine that you are releasing any stress or tension from anywhere in your body. Keep breathing in this manner, inhaling cleansing breath and exhaling tension and stress.

- When you feel relaxed, create in your mind an image of the person standing against a blank background. Notice as many details as you can about him or her: clothing, hair, and general demeanor. Notice the facial expression. Open your eyes and draw your impression of the person on a piece of paper. As you draw you can add detail to your initial impressions.

- Now, draw yourself facing your person at about an arm's distance. Pay attention to any feelings that surface as you do this (laughing at your drawing doesn't count).

- Close your eyes and, starting at the top of your head, scan your body. As your awareness moves down your body, imagine that there are invisible connectors that run from part of your body to a part of the other person's body. Take note of which parts are connected. There may be more than one.

- Pick the connector that feels strongest, and imagine what it seems to be made of—a steel rod, a fleshy appendage, a vibration of light, a rope. Does there seem to be energy flowing through this connector? If so, which direction is it flowing? Do your best to tune in to the energy flow through the connector. When you feel as if you have received as much information as you can, open your eyes and make a sketch of the connectors, putting emphasis on the connector that felt the strongest. If you did not receive much information, use your imagination and just draw what feels right.

- You now have the opportunity to release this connector. Close your eyes, and imagine that you have the power to disconnect yourself from your person. You may want to ask for divine guidance and intervention in order to let go. The other person may resist your letting go of the connector. You might feel as if it is unloving to let go, or you may feel as if you need this connector in order to keep this person in your life. Do not judge or fear what will happen when you disconnect from this person. Let go. When you do let go, don't be surprised if you feel sad, fearful, angry, or unkind. Those feelings are not unusual.

- Once you have disconnected, take the connector and imagine you are attaching it to the highest source of absolute love. Allow this love to flow through you, especially into the areas where the connector was originally attached.

- Release your person to absolute love.

- Open your eyes and tear or cut the paper in half, separating you from your person. Then, glue your image to a separate piece of paper and add pictures of beauty, abundance, and love. If you like, you can add the image of the now-separate person, with abundance, happiness, and love pictures surrounding you both.

- Allowing your intuition to guide you, you might write an affirmation on the paper, such as "I attract absolute love" or "I am worthy of love and abundance."

- If you wish, you could glue your now-separated person to a different piece of paper. Add pictures or images that you feel will help and empower him or her.

Kristine

When Kristine did this exercise she immediately tuned in to a connector that she created with Steven from her heart and energy field. She realized that she was sending him waves of love and spiritual energy. Kristine was at first reluctant to release this connector. She knew that she had much love to give and felt it important that she continue to do so. As she sat with these feelings, she had the sudden intuitive knowing that as long as she kept bolstering Steven in this manner he would not look within himself for the divine source of love. He would depend on her. She understood in a flash that this was keeping him from developing and being able to share with her as a spiritual equal.

Kristine also became aware of the connection she had with Steven in the lower part of her body. These connectors felt strong, like metal. There was an impressive flow of energy that ran from Steven to her, and it surprised her. She was struck with the realization that she was completely materially and financially dependent on Steven. She knew she was not growing or challenging herself but was expecting him to be the financially responsible partner.

She imagined disconnecting from Steven and allowing absolute love to flow through her. She invited his energy into this healing and encouraged his spirit to accept the love that was being offered to him. She asked her angels and his to continue to heal and guide them. She knew that this was different from the love that she had been giving him. She could feel the freedom that this love offered them both.

What to Expect

People are often surprised at how effective this exercise can be. We often underestimate the power of our energetic actions and intent. The subject of your exercise will always feel the energetic disconnection at some level. The subject will sense a change, and it is likely that he or she will try to reestablish the old patterns, begin to cling, feel insecure, or become manipulative. Or, the person may leave the relationship altogether. Don't be surprised if you feel unsure or question your resolve. It is normal to experience feelings of uncertainty before a new pattern of relating is established.

You will, however, feel an invigorating flow of energy. You now have the power of choice. Choose wisely, and avoid the temptation to ignore your deficits or areas that still need growth and encouragement. Confront your fears and insecurities, whatever that entails. Commit to the path of love.

14

HEALING
SPIRITUAL CODEPENDENCE

∿∿∿∿∿∿∿∿∿∿∿∿∿∿∿∿∿∿∿∿∿∿∿

What's love got to do with it? Here's another question: What's the energy field have to do with it? It might be difficult to comprehend how something as elusive and abstract as the energy field, or aura, can impact your love relationships. But it can and it does.

It is easy to underestimate the importance of the energy field because, under normal circumstances, we cannot see, feel, or measure it. We naturally question whether or not the energy field or aura is even real. Yet your energy field can both magnetize and draw to you an abundance of love or attract into your life all kinds of difficulties and anguish.

Your Aura in Love

As intuition develops, so does your sensitivity to energy. You can tune in to your energy field by imagining it as a luminous web of light that completely encircles you. Imagine that sparks of constantly moving, clear radiance envelope you, and threads of light extend from the orb that surrounds you. These threads of light reach into realms of vibrant absolute love energy. Your body, cells, heart, and mind are nourished by the flowing inter-connectedness of the human aura with vibrations of absolute love. Threads of light reach out to your friends, loved ones, and even strangers. Your light seeks playful union with others. When your light sparks meet another's light sparks, a joyful explosion of love occurs in you.

The Shadow

Imagine in the web of light there are also shadows and dark places that refuse to join the flow of love. Maybe the dark places are fearful of the light, and they contract and hold their ground. These dark places can also reach out to the dark places in others. When this happens, they too grow stronger and take up more energy and space, but they are stuck and heavy, and they weigh you down.

The dark places in your energy field are your fears, judgments, and emotional wounds. When your energy field connects with others through these shadow spots instead of through light, the stage is set for spiritual codependence. We often reach out to others in the expectation that they can make us happy or fill us with love. It is, however, only through the awareness of the love within us that our love expands.

Limiting Love

Spiritual codependence typically leaves you feeling tired, drained, and overwhelmed. In a spiritual codependent relationship, spiritual and emotional growth is sabotaged, intuitive receptivity is squelched, and the free flow of unconditional and compassionate love is stifled. It occurs when you establish a relationship that compensates for one another's needs and limitations, and consequently you cut yourself off from higher life-force energy. In a spiritual codependent relationship the energy field is in an energetic gridlock, and growth and evolution stall.

Trouble in Paradise

To understand how the energy field can affect a relationship, we revisit Kristine and Steven. When they first met, Kristine and Steven felt fortunate that their personality likes and dislikes balanced one another. Kristine was highly spiritual and creative, and Steven was well grounded and driven in his career. Together, they reasoned, they made a perfect couple. But what seemed like Nirvana at first soon turned into an atmosphere of resentment and frustration.

Steven was devoted to his job, and Kristine was caught up in her spiritual and creative endeavors. While she very much enjoyed the time she had to pursue her passions, she was often lonely and tired. With his life so full of work responsibilities, Steven began to envy Kristine's carefree approach to life. He became despondent and angry.

Kristine took the first steps in healing by energetically detaching from her dependence on Steven's grounded and practical approach to life. She also transformed her impulse to overcompensate for his lack of emotional and spiritual growth by inviting the higher vibrations of absolute love into the relationship. When she was able to tune in to the stuck energetic pattern that she had formed with Steven and devote herself to healing the imbalances, their marriage began to change. Kristine felt stronger and more open to new possibilities. She no longer energetically supported Steven's emotional and spiritual needs and thus had more energy and stamina to devote to her own healing and growth. She pursued her desire to become a yoga instructor and committed to a year-long training course. She also enrolled in a holistic health seminar to see if that might be a possible career path for her.

Steven was not so excited about these changes. He felt different, but he didn't know why. While he understood Kristine's interest in developing a career and was outwardly supportive of it, he felt abandoned and unloved. He felt as if she didn't need him anymore, and he started to feel insecure and suspicious. He didn't know how to communicate his needs to Kristine, because he was barely able to recognize that he had any. He picked a few arguments with her in an attempt to get her attention. But this only made him feel worse. He blamed Kristine for their problems, suggested a trial separation, and moved into an apartment.

Very quickly, Steven began to miss Kristine and her enthusiasm and zest for life. He became uninterested in work and was barely able to make it through his day. He sunk into a depression, and seemed to have no energy. He remembered when he first met Kristine, how just being near her energized him. Even though he didn't share her spiritual interests, he had been attracted to her because of her pure belief in the divine. She could feel her angels, and she believed in a loving and supportive universe. Now, he felt abandoned by her and had no trust or faith in life to fall back on. He was empty, and life had no meaning.

The Hidden Dependence

Kristine and Steven were stuck in a spiritual codependent relationship. Without knowing it, Steven depended on Kristine for his life-force energy. Kristine's dependence on Steven was more obvious; she relied on him to pay the bills and manage their everyday lives. Steven needed the healing waves of love that naturally emanated from Kristine's well-developed, spiritual nature; without this he felt depressed and without purpose.

Spiritual codependence is a common energetic and spiritual relationship imbalance. Codependency describes a relationship addiction. It is the over-focusing on the needs and behaviors of others and giving over your power and sense of self in an attempt to fulfill or fix another. It is sacrificing your own needs by giving too much energy, time, and attention to another in an attempt to feel better about yourself. Codependence is also expecting that another can completely fulfill your needs as well as depending on another's moods and feelings in order to feel good about yourself. Spiritual codependence not only affects you emotionally, but spiritually and energetically as well.

How Spiritual Codependence Develops

Spiritual codependence usually begins in childhood. Unfortunately, most of us are taught to love from a material perspective. We are told through the unconscious paradigm of the world that we must compete for love and abundance. We learn to live in a state of compromise, believing that we must repress our empowered spirit in order to excel in the competitive world of school and sports, and in the social and economic environment of our future.

Our parents and the environment are our role models for how to love ourselves. As children, we tune in to our parents' psychic environment. We are connected to their energy fields, and we receive unspoken energetic lessons about how to be in relationships with others. We are influenced by our parents' love energy, not only how they love us but also how they love themselves. Because many people are not conscious of their own spiritual, love-centered nature, they are unable to offer it to their children. The spiritual truth that we are whole and pure loving beings is seldom integrated into our emotional energy as children.

Spiritual codependence is likely the most common energetic imbalance that affects our relationships. It is similar to emotional codependence in that it keeps us looking outside of ourselves for a sense of fulfillment. The spiritual codependent seeks necessary life-force energy from others or allows others to consume his or her own. Its origin is in lack of awareness of the energetic spirit self or the inability to consciously connect with it.

The Desire to Become One
Spiritual codependence is divine reality gone haywire. In the spiritual realms as we ascend into the higher vibrations, we naturally merge with other similar and harmonious energies.

The tendency to desire this kind of merged union in the material and physical world is deeply ingrained within us. It is natural that we would want to bond completely with those we love. Yet when we attempt to depend on others as our primary spiritual source, we cripple our spirit and energetically suffocate those we care about. When we look to the material world for those things for which the soul yearns, we create an inner void and emptiness. We are dissociated from our multidimensional self.

Oneness and unification with one another are reality in the spiritual realms. When we seek this unity on the material plane, without a core sense and awareness of our innate inner spirit, spiritual codependence is the result. We are fragmented, and we live through our most unenlightened aspects.

Psychic Vampires

Spiritual codependence creates a number of energetic and psychic disturbances. When you are not connected to this nurturing source, you wither like a branch cut from a tree. Your energy field becomes weak and repressed, which may unconsciously cause you to attempt to draw energy from others or your environment. We use the term *psychic vampire* to describe people who seek energy from outside of themselves in order to feel strong, alive, and healthy. Yet, attaching to another's energy field in a desire to feel whole is never satisfying for long. This is, at best, a temporary fix, one that keeps you in a constantly dependent state.

On the other end is the person who allows others to draw energy from him or her. This unconscious pattern, too, most likely develops in childhood. It can occur when parents look to their children for their own sense of purpose and fulfillment. The child grows up to expect, and allows, others to draw energy from him. As adults, these children are usually tired, depleted, and may avoid the company of others so as to keep from feeling drained or even ill.

Intuition and Spiritual Codependency
Another symptom of spiritual codependency is repressed intuitive functioning. Your intuition, like your other senses, is an innate and natural part of you. Intuitive sensing is the awareness of subtle vibrations that your five senses cannot perceive. When you are consciously connected to your inner spiritual core, your intuition can come into its full expression.

Spiritual codependence affects your ability to connect with your natural intuition. Natural intuitive sensors become silenced when you lack pure life-force energy, and you become overwhelmed with influences from the material world. You are unable to hear your intuitive inner voice. When you are cut off from intuitive knowing, you can feel as if you are living in a haze of meaningless, chance circumstances. You have difficulty trusting your attractions to others, and you may feel unconnected to those you love and care about. You have no inner sensor guiding you to what will bring joy and purpose.

You may also become overwhelmed with the energy of others and of your environment, unknowingly soaking in toxins and negativity.

Being continuously merged with another's energy field creates confusion, inner chaos, stress, negativity, and anxiety.

When your body intuitively receives the energy of others, you may become ill, tired, and stressed, and take on the aches and pains of your loved ones. To protect yourself from being overwhelmed by the energy of others and the environment, you may tend to avoid intimacy and its risk of vulnerability. This avoidance itself can lead to depression and increased loneliness.

The following are common symptoms of spiritual codependence:

- Chronic tiredness
- Lack of trust in the nonphysical realms
- Depression
- No awareness of your own intuitive functioning
- Need to be in another's physical presence in order to feel connected to him or her
- Inability to perceive meaning in the mundane
- Life events feel random and inconsequential
- View imagination as fanciful and meaningless
- Feel as if others need your energy in order to feel the presence of a higher power
- Unable to believe something is real unless it is perceived through the five senses
- Fear of the unknown
- Constant need to protect yourself from the unseen
- Allow others to deplete you energetically
- Feeling powerless

- Unable to make positive changes in your life
- Belief that your contributions to life are trivial
- Feelings of being special or more worthy of a higher power's love and intercession
- Belief that your spiritual/intuitive gifts make you special
- Desire to use spiritual/intuitive gifts to gain control or power over others
- Not sharing your spirituality with those closest to you
- Need relationships to feel energized
- Power is felt as control, manipulation, or force

Spiritual Codependence by Type

Spiritual codependence affects each intuitive type in distinct ways. When the energy field is not open to the vital life-force energy of absolute love, then the primary energy that one intuits is from the mundane level of relative love. This creates an energetic imbalance that keeps one at the mercy of the ups and downs of relative love. It is in the energy of absolute love that we access the higher states of joy, healing, and positivity.

Physical Intuitives

For the physical intuitive, spiritual codependence keeps one looking to the physical and material realm to fulfill one's emotional and spiritual needs. Because physical intuitives intuit energy through their physical body, when their intuitive receptors are not open to the higher realms of absolute love, they become easily overwhelmed with worldly toxins. This can cause them to become numb or hypersensitive to touch and physical closeness. They can feel stressed or physically depleted, and lack stamina.

In intimate relationships they may experience an endless desire for sexual experience or its opposite, physical apathy and no sexual drive. Either way one is left feeling unconnected to others and longing for intimacy.

Emotional Intuitives

Emotional intuitives will often be unable to process emotions, their own and those that they intuit from others. They are likely to get stuck in feelings of anger, resentment, fear, or depression. On an intuitive level they are likely to attract and receive these same negative emotions from others. Like attracts like; another law of the universe dictates that we will intuit from others and the environment the feelings and emotions that we most experience. Unfortunately, this only adds to the emotional stress that the emotional intuitive already feels. In relationships they may as a result become overemotional, difficult to please, needy, and dramatic. They may be on an endless and unsatisfying search for an idealistic love that can give them the emotional high that they crave.

Mental Intuitives

Spiritual codependence for the mental intuitive is the inability to break through patterns of negative and often obsessive thinking. They may be unable to move out of their own perspective, and the mental energy that they intuit from the environment will reinforce their own bias.

Negative thought forms are a collective mass of energy, that like a fungus feeds on itself and constantly regenerates and grows. People who are unable to open to the inspiring, creative, and loving thoughts of the universe often attract negative thought forms. This becomes a prison, where they are trapped in dark thoughts, beliefs, and attitudes.

In relationships the mental intuitive caught in this negative shadow may become obsessed with a particular person, thought, or belief. They are apt to want their partner to always agree with them, and they often seek to control and manipulate the thoughts and beliefs of those whom they are close to.

Spiritual Intuitives

You may be wondering, "Can a spiritual intuitive be closed off to spiritual energy?" The simple answer is yes and no—okay, maybe it's not so simple. Spiritual intuitives intuit energy primarily through their energy field. When they are not open to the beneficial flow of vital life-force energy, they primarily receive energy vibrations that are emitted from the etheric level. The etheric level of energy is the first subtle layer of energy which surrounds the physical body. It acts as a go-between for the physical body and the higher emanations of vital life-force energy.

The spiritual intuitive who is not soaking in the rich life-giving energy of the higher realms develops acute sensitivity to sounds, smells, and light. They become hypersensitive in relationships and may respond in confusing ways. Subtle moods, emotions, and behaviors from their partner often trigger a fight-or-flight response, and because of their baffling acute sensitivities they may forgo intimacy altogether and instead end up in superficial and short-term relationships.

Healing Spiritual Codependency

A healthy energy field is open, translucent, and continuously nurtured by a flowing circuit of vital energy. Like a plant that seeks life from the sun and rain, our spirit relies upon its connection with a potent source of absolute love and wisdom. The source of this nurturing is the center of love and life-force energy itself.

The scientific community accepts the presence of different types of energy, such as heat, light, nuclear, chemical, gravitational, and kinetic, among others. So in the spiritual, religious, and metaphysical communities there is acceptance of vital, life-giving energy, referred to by such names as the Holy Spirit, etheric energy, universal life force, quantum energy, Great Spirit, essence, and the Light. In Sanskrit, this fundamental and essential energy is called *prana*. In Chinese it is referred to as *qi* or *chi'i*. In most ancient systems of healing, this energy is believed to be essential for health and well-being.

Not only is your body nurtured by this high vibration of energy, but your energy field is as well. When your energy field is fully functional you are less likely to form unhealthy energetic alliances and are less likely to feel drained when in the company of others. The energy field, bolstered by vital energy, naturally repels all that is not in a similar, positive unison with it. You have no need to attach to others, and therefore you are more able to make positive and affirming relationship choices. When you make the decision to attune to heightened levels of energy, your spiritual codependence can be healed.

Psychic Cleansing

The following exercise can help release and transform any stress, tension, or negativity in your body and energy field. When your consciousness is attuned to healing loving energy, you thrive.

By practicing this meditation often, you can train your energy field to naturally seek its nurturance and stamina from a higher source. As a result you will flow in the natural current of life-force energy. You will be empowered to give and receive love, and your intuitive channels will be clear and strong.

To begin, sit or lie in a comfortable position, and begin to relax. You may want to pray, meditate, or ask for the white light of protection. The impressions that you receive may be images, feelings, thoughts, smells, symbols, and bodily sensations.

- Close your eyes and take a deep breath; release this breath and take another long, deep breath. Take a few more cleansing breaths, releasing and relaxing. With each inhale and exhale you release more and more stress or tension anywhere in your body. Continue this relaxing breathing for as long as you like.

- Imagine that surrounding your body is a translucent rainbow of light and color. You are continuously bathed in this rich stream of absolute love, vibration, and energy. Relax, and allow these colors and vibrations to surround you.

- Expand your consciousness from within your body outward to the energy surrounding you. Imagine expanding into this vibrant rainbow of light and love.

- Now draw your awareness to the top of your head and breathe in white-light love energy. As you do, you may feel this breath as a tingling sensation; allow love to flow through you.

- Become conscious of a spiral of energy surrounding your head. Breathe white-light love into this area. Imagine your third eye opening. Deep purples and indigo may appear. Continue to breathe energy and love into this area, releasing any negativity, stress, and tension. Imagine your consciousness expanding into bliss.

- Move your awareness to the throat area. Imagine white-light love flowing into this area. Allow the light to dissolve and release whatever you no longer need. Allow the inner voice of truth to emerge. Listen and breathe.

- Become aware of your heart. Imagine rich waves of absolute love opening within you; expand into this love. Become a conduit for the healing energy of love. Allow any hidden pain, wound, or grief to surface. Feel your feelings, however difficult they may be. Know that all you need to do to let go of difficult feelings is to feel them as they surface. Commit to loving yourself.

- Become aware of your solar plexus; feel its strength and vibrancy. Allow love to flow into your stomach. Feel the presence of truth within you. Breathe and release any shame or guilt. Imagine love as the ability to be in your truth. Feel the power of absolute love as grace, love, and compassion.

- Move your consciousness into the area below your belly button. Breathe energy and love into this area. Release and let go of any limiting judgments about your sexuality and ability to thrive in a relationship. Clear this area with the breath of love. Send the energy of love to all areas of your life. Invite the absolute love into the mundane aspects of your life, and commit to the manifestation of your highest good.

- Become aware of the base of your spine. Breathe love into this area and feel your connection with the earth. Feel the earth supporting and loving you. The earth has called you into physical being. It loves you and supports you. Send love to the earth and all of her creatures. Feel your oneness with all that is.

- Allow love to flow through your entire body. It has intelligence and vibrancy. It flows to all the places in your body that have been tight or tense. Those places that have held pain or negativity now open to the healing lightness of love. This light lifts and dissolves all that is not in your highest good, filling you with love. This love continues to spread throughout your body, relaxing and energizing you. This love extends itself about twelve inches from your body, forming an orb of white light that completely surrounds you and allows stress and negativity to exit, but only that which is in your highest good to enter.

- Now imagine that within you there is a deep, infinite well. Allow the light to enter and fill this space with love. Imagine that you have within you a gold mine of richness and splendor. It whispers to you that you are love. There is an endless supply of love at your beck and call. Immerse yourself in love for as long as possible.

- When you are ready, open your eyes and write down any thoughts, impressions, visions, or feelings you experienced. Do not try to understand or think too much about what you felt or experienced; just let it go, knowing that you are being healed at a deep level.

This meditation will allow you to experience the natural flow of absolute love and life-giving energy. One unexpected benefit of spiritual healing is that deep patterns of negativity or dysfunction can be healed spontaneously. This kind of healing is not conditioned by time and space. When your energy system is cleared and cleansed, surprising changes and shifts are likely to occur in your life.

Healing through Intuitive Type

Each psychic type—mental, emotional, spiritual, and physical—has its own spiritual strengths upon which to draw for further healing of spiritual codependence. Everyone can benefit from these healing suggestions. Practice those to which you feel most drawn.

Mental Intuitives

Acknowledge instances of synchronicity or meaningful coincidence in everyday matters. These may surface through numbers, ideas, or technology. Meditate on merging your consciousness with the divine mind, also called the superconsciousness.

When flowing with the energy of absolute love, mental intuitives align with compassionate wisdom. They bring understanding, keen insight, and the ability to discern the lessons, meaning, and purpose in their life and in the life of those they love.

Their intuition refines itself into telepathy and the ability to foresee the progression and unfolding of events and patterns.

Emotional Intuitives
Acknowledge the divine in yourself and others. Become aware of when you are absorbing the emotional energy of others, and instead set the intention that a higher healing love move through you to them. Meditate on heart expansion, and open your heart to receive the highest vibrations of love.

As emotional intuitives refine their intuitive gifts, they develop the ability to heal others through empathetic insight and forgiveness. They become a divine conduit for the unconditional power of absolute love.

Emotional intuitives bring to their relationships devotion, emotional wisdom, and heart-centered perception.

Spiritual Intuitives
Visualize the energy field of yourself, your friends, family, and even strangers, and imagine it surrounded by love as white-light energy. Keep a dream journal. Contemplate your purpose

and mission while here on earth. Pray and meditate for healing for others.

Energized with absolute love, the spiritual intuitive is like a majestic and free eagle, soaring to the heights of love's ethereal limits and bringing this love to the mundane everyday world. They can lift those they love into this bliss and ecstatic inspiration.

Their refined intuitive gifts are clairvoyance, often called *second sight*, or the ability to see the unseen and the ability to communicate and commune with the higher realms—angels, guides, and loved ones.

Physical Intuitives

Contemplate the divine in all living things. Feel the life-force energy inherent in all of nature, including the animal, plant, and mineral realms. Meditate on your oneness and connection with all of life. Spend quiet time alone in nature.

Absolute love is vibrant and powerful energy when it flows from a physical intuitive. You can feel it oozing from their pores and in their presence you will safe and well loved. Their touch, when aligned with absolute love, will heal you, relax you, and send you into sensual erotic pleasure.

Their refined intuitive gifts are the ability to heal through touch, communicate with earth spirits and animals, and create through magic and ritual.

Instant Healing

We all suffer from spiritual codependence, some of us in a more extreme form than others. The world that we live in has long denied the existence and power of spiritual energy, so it has been easy to deny our need for this connection. The good news is that, when addressed, spiritual codependence can be healed quickly, often instantaneously. The rich benevolent flow of universal life-force energy is always available to you. Despite your past, your sense of self, or the condition that you find yourself in, open to the healing rays of a higher love, and heal.

15

INTERACT WITH YOUR PSYCHIC INNER CHILD

~~~~~~

There is a magical innocent spirit within you that longs to come out and play. The emergence of this inner childlike aspect is often invoked through the healing of spiritual codependence. This part of your multidimensional nature, which I call the *inner psychic child*, can be a powerful source of intuitive knowing, fun, and a great ally in attracting and sustaining loving and passionate relationships.

Living in Two Worlds

Your birth into this world is a journey from boundless freedom and space into limitation. You come into the physical realm with a script of lessons, purpose, and karma to experience. Yet the soul always resides in love and wisdom. It is the inner psychic child who bridges the gap between the spiritual and the material. Often muffled and quieted by the conditioning of the material world, the psychic inner child is always with you. Although I refer to this aspect of your total being as a child, it is both timeless and childlike in its openness to love and connection to joy.

The psychic inner child resides in the realms of all possibility and freedom. This aspect of your nature is naturally psychic in that it lives outside of time, space, and physical limitations. As you become more aware of the psychic inner child, your intuition is infused with energy, wisdom, and love.

The psychic inner child views the world as a creative and curious playground.

Integrating this aspect of your being into your conscious life increases your ability to play, share, and freely give and receive love.

Steven

Steven, our spiritual codependent, relied for years on the positive flow of vital energy to which his wife, Kristine, was naturally connected. He had not developed his own conscious connection to his inner spirit or resources, so he did not know how to access inner guidance and absolute love energy. When Steven and Kristine separated, he became even more depressed and lost. Being a mental intuitive, he thought incessantly about their last few conversations and searched his mind for insight as to what had happened and why.

Kristine, a spiritual intuitive, continued to apply herself to her yoga training and other holistic classes, and she was able to find a part-time administrative job at the yoga center. She knew that being married to Steven made it easy for her to ignore the important growth that she needed to make in grounding her spiritual gifts and fulfilling her purpose.

She still loved Steven. She knew he was lonely and that he blamed her for his unhappiness. Every morning before she started her busy day, Kristine would meditate and pray. She would send love to Steven and visualize him wrapped in loving, white light. She would ask his angels to help him find his way. Kristine missed Steven, and she was sad and at times angry but continued on with taking care of herself.

Steven continued to suffer. He was unhappy at work and didn't know how to make changes in his life. One night in the midst of his discontent, he had a dream that he was in the mountains of Colorado with his now-deceased grandfather. They were laughing and fishing in a favorite vacation spot from his boyhood. When Steven awoke, he was more at peace than he had been for a long time. He went into work that morning and, without much thought, scheduled some vacation days. He was going to Colorado. That evening he packed his gear and made reservations at a rustic campground; the next day he was in the mountains.

For the next several days Steven hiked and fished, and he started to relax. He loved these mountains; he loved the pure, fresh air and the sound of the river tumbling over the rocks. One evening as he quietly stared into his campfire, he dozed off and, in a half-asleep state, he recalled that as a boy he would often see visions of Native Americans in this area. He felt he could sense their presence again. He had been a quiet, introverted only child, and the spirits were his playmates; they comforted him. Tears rolled down his cheeks as he wondered if these spirits were real and might help him now. He sent out a message into the pine-scented air and the rolling hills, "Please help me now!"

The next morning Steven awoke with renewed enthusiasm and began to explore the beautiful environment, but something in him had changed. The plants and flowers, even the sky and water, seemed to be alive and vibrant. He felt the curiosity and wonder of his younger years. There was a magical being within him that guided and encouraged him. He felt he could communicate with the spirit world. Every living thing had something to say to him, and he had a renewed sense of being part of the greater whole, connected, and at peace. He was alive again.

Each day his heart seemed to open just a little bit more, and for the first time in quite a while he felt feelings of love move through him. He realized that somewhere along the way of career focus and making money he had lost a part of himself. He had never really valued his own spirit and had begun to resent Kristine for her willingness to nurture hers. "How sad," he now thought, "I walked away from the most valuable part of life, my own spirit, and my extraordinary wife."

A few weeks later, back at home, Steven called Kristine and asked her to meet with him. The following day Kristine saw Steven standing near the edge of a fast-moving river waiting for her at the agreed-upon spot in their favorite park. When Kristine saw Steven her heart seemed to skip a beat. He looked different from the way he had just a few weeks earlier. He had a look of contentment on his face. Gone were the stress lines and furrowed brow. He greeted her with a warm smile, and they spent the next few hours talking about Steven's recent trip to Colorado. It was evident to Kristine that Steven had a renewed sense of purpose and connection with life. As Steven shared his experiences, Kristine felt herself encouraged and ready to begin the process of healing their marriage.

Recognizing the Psychic Inner Child

In order to become aware of your psychic inner child, you must accept your own pure spirit. We have been taught by our culture to devalue our spiritual, childlike innocence, so we misjudge it as weak and impractical. When you were young you may have been told that life is serious business, and to be safe and happy you must become a tough and resilient. There was little use for the wistful wisdom of your ethereal reality.

The idea of embracing the psychic inner child can feel frivolous and impractical. You will find, though, that connecting with the psychic inner child leads you back to your core essence. Your psychic inner child retains the richness of the soul, and playfully dangles it in front of your world-weary eyes. This child does not want to live in a world without love and laughter. Its presence in your life is an invitation into imaging and lightheartedness. We see the world as solid and quantifiable; the child sees it as an environment of creativity and possibilities.

Contacting Your Psychic Inner Child

The following exercise provides you the opportunity to reconnect with your psychic inner child. It is important to go into this exercise with a childlike sense of fun and imagination.

Lie or sit down in a comfortable position and close your eyes. Take a few deep, relaxing breaths. Inhale cleansing breaths and exhale any stress or tension in the body.

- Continue to breathe and open your heart.

- Send a message to your psychic inner child that you would like to connect with him or her. Breathe into your heart, and send your psychic inner child the message that you would like to know more about him or her.

- Imagine a triangle. Notice its color, texture, and any other details. Imagine the triangle as an energy portal.

- Imagine that your psychic inner child's energy is present in the center of the triangle. If you do not readily see or feel a presence, actively use your imagination to create an image that represents your psychic inner child. Your psychic inner child may play with you. Instead of seeing a child, you may see a symbol, an animal, a magical scene, a unicorn—the possibilities are endless. Accept whatever emerges.

- Take a few moments to tune in to the energy of your psychic inner child. Let the images change and evolve. The scene may have a playful quality.

- Open your eyes when you are ready and write down everything that you experienced.

Emotional intuitives may feel the initial emergence of the psychic inner child through feelings of pleasure, laughter, or good-natured rebelliousness. Their psychic inner child will enjoy bringing pleasure to others and expressing feelings and emotions through dance, drawing, and all kinds of creative play.

Mental intuitives may receive insight from the psychic inner child about all kinds of things, both frivolous and practical. Their psychic inner child may want them to investigate cutting-edge "New Age" inventions, faraway planetary systems, and extraterrestrials. They may also enjoy science fiction and fantasy.

For physical intuitives it is a good idea to tune in to any sensations or gut feelings. This might be a tingling feeling throughout the body and a joyful heart expansion. Their psychic inner child may want to romp through the natural world and marvel at plants, stones, clouds, and natural beauty in all forms. They will easily communicate with animals and nature spirits, and they are likely to enjoy magic.

Spiritual intuitives may go on an imaginative adventure with their psychic inner child to different realms full of curious creatures and spirit companions. Their psychic inner child will help them to see auras, and introduce them to the angelic realm, fairies, and other supernatural companions.

My Psychic Inner Child's Encouragement

My psychic inner child has become a potent force of positivity in my relationships. Being a psychic and a single woman has its challenges. When I tell other people that I'm a psychic, their expression immediately changes. Their look may be one of mild curiosity, sheer horror, disbelief, or "get me out of here right now!" There are those who feel immediately comfortable with me, but unfortunately they are not the norm.

Dating has not been easy. For a long time when I was asked in social situations about my profession I used terms like *spiritual counselor*, *intuitive mentor*, *coach*, or *spiritual therapist*. This word-play was not helpful. I felt I lacked integrity, and that is who I attracted—people who themselves were not comfortable with who they were.

My psychic inner child tells me that "I am who I am, and I do what I do." She tells me to be more of me and to have fun. She reminds me that I do not have to search for love or find someone to love me. I have all the love I need—right inside of me. When I see her, she is often dancing in a shower of light and encouraging me to enthusiastically share myself with others. The conventional dating approaches don't really work. We attract a partner by following our bliss, and finding out what it is in life that helps us to open our hearts—and then sharing it with others. My psychic inner child is always there with an open heart, ready to spread the joy.

Tarot Card Adventures

An adventure that will call your psychic inner child out is to go to a bookstore that carries a large selection of tarot cards. Communicate to your child that you would like it to select a deck of cards. Most likely it will indicate a choice through a feeling of laughter and smiles as you search through the various decks. If you feel analytical or burdened with the options, it is not your psychic inner child at work. When you feel a sense of lightness with a certain deck, buy it. Do not read about it or ask the salesclerk's or anyone else's opinion. Just buy it. Take the cards home and look through them. Again, do not read about them or try to interpret their meaning.

Your psychic inner child can be very helpful when it comes to relationships, especially love relationships. It can see into the spirit and intent of others with uncanny accuracy. Your psychic inner child can communicate and give you messages about your relationship with particular people through the tarot cards.

Try this: Pick out a tarot card that represents you and a card that represents the person you are asking about. Kings, queens, knights, and pages make good choices for this exercise.

Shuffle the cards and think of a question for your psychic inner child. When you feel you are ready, cut the cards with your nondominant hand. Turn over the top card, and look at it. Then ask your psychic inner child to help you understand its meaning. Sit quietly and listen to whatever surfaces. Guidance may come to you as a thought, a feeling, or a knowing, or you may hear an inner message. Write down in your journal whatever you receive. You can continue with this exercise, always asking a question of the psychic inner child, cutting the cards with the nondominant hand, and listening quietly. When you feel as if you have received as much information from your inner child as possible, read from other card-interpretation sources that pique your interest.

A variation of this exercise is to spread the cards face down on a table, and with your nondominant hand hold a hanging crystal pendulum over them. Ask the pendulum to show you what a yes response looks like and then ask for a no response. When you feel confident that you are getting reliable responses, hold the pendulum over small sections of the cards until you receive a yes response. Then turn the card over and be open to whatever comes to you in thought or emotion.

Your psychic inner child might play games with you to test and see if it can trust you. You may find that the cards frustrate or confuse you. Know that quite often the psychic inner child has been denied for so long that it may surface with a bit of a fuss. If you feel as if you are trying too hard to understand the cards, take a break. Go for a walk, play with a pet, or do something else you enjoy. Often the voice of our psychic inner child will be easier to hear when we are relaxed and having fun.

Be patient and continue—eventually trust will be established, and it will become your most reliable source of insight and truth.

Stream of Consciousness Writing
You might also want to use the technique of nondominant-hand writing to tap into the energy of your psychic inner child. Simply write down a question with your dominant hand. Then with your nondominant hand, write whatever comes to you, without censoring or overthinking. It will feel clumsy and childlike to write with your nondominant hand, but keep writing. The psychic inner child will at some point begin to write through you. You can receive very valuable intuitive insights with this exercise.

Amber
Amber is a client of mine whose unexpected encounter with her inner psychic child opened the door to positive relation-

ship growth. Amber has been on a conscious path of inner healing and growth for many years. She met Dave, a musician and writer, at a friend's house. They talked all night and began dating the next day. Amber told me that one of the traits that she appreciated most about Dave was his sense of fun and spontaneity. He traveled quite a bit, and together they planned ski, snorkeling, and kayaking trips.

Amber was excited by all of their plans but came to see me one day feeling anxious and stressed. She told me that as much as she was looking forward to their upcoming weekend rafting trip, she was also petrified. She had grown up with alcoholic parents whose constant fighting created a stressful and anxious home environment. Amber, without realizing it, sought control in her relationships and activities, and the thought of being in a small craft coursing down a turbulent river was almost too much for her. She trusted Dave and wanted to participate, but she was becoming increasingly fearful.

Amber felt like she needed to relax and asked me to help her to perceive the upcoming weekend in a more positive way. I had her close her eyes, breathe, and visualize a calm and serene environment. As she went into a deep and quiet meditative state, a vibrant young and magical Amber suddenly appeared in her mind's eye. This Amber was full of life and ready for any adventure. She was looking forward to spending time in nature and her enthusiasm was infectious. Grown-up Amber was at first a bit put off by her exuberance; however, when an image of inner psychic child Amber confidently steering her way down the river emerged, she was intrigued. Almost as if on cue, another image soon appeared of Amber standing on the front porch of a house hand in hand with Dave, while two young children contentedly played in the yard. The scene was so real that the knot in her stomach gave way and warm pleasure moved through her body. She felt she could trust the inner-psychic Amber to lead her into this vision, and so she sat up and told me she was ready. She could ride the river.

Continued Connection

As you begin to nurture and accept the energy of your psychic inner child, there will be increased moments of clear recognition of his or her presence. Your psychic inner child can become a powerful ally that you will likely grow to depend upon for uncanny relationship advice. They have a way of seeing beyond appearances and into the truth of another's character and intent. Invoking their presence will invigorate your intuitive development, with energy and fun.

PART III
Intimate Intuitive Love

16

BECOME A
SOUL-MATE MAGNET

Among the most common questions I am asked during a psychic reading are those having to do with finding love. The search for a deep and loving relationship can make one a bit anxious. "Where and when will I meet my soul mate?" "What does he look like?" "Do I even have a soul mate?" "How do I know if my new girlfriend is the 'one'?"

We are overly concerned with "being in the right place at the right time," fearful that one false move might leave us loveless for a lifetime. We tend to operate under the belief that there is a limited supply of love, and there are maybe just one, two, or perhaps a few souls who can truly love us.

While it is tempting to feel powerless when it comes to attracting a loving partner, please remember this truth: *Conditions conform to your readiness to receive.* When you are ready to open your heart and invite your soul mate into your life, he or she will enter. You have power. Your intuition can help you to invite this person into your life and recognize your soul mate.

The Problem of Safety

Elsie

Elsie consulted me last fall, wondering if she would ever meet her soul mate. She had been on a few dates in the past year, but she had not felt a strong attraction to any of the men that she had met. She wanted a partner with whom she felt a deep, loving, and intimate connection. As I began her reading, I was touched by the warmth and love that I could sense within her. The problem seemed to be that she was hiding her natural loving nature behind a sturdy, protective shell. She did not want to appear vulnerable, and she was afraid of rejection. She did not want to risk being hurt or deceived, so she hid behind a calm and in-control façade. But like the sun blocked by heavy clouds, her warmth and light was unexpressed. Because of her reluctance to reveal her inner soulful self, Elsie attracted superficial men and shallow, unfulfilling, short-term relationships.

Our Longing for Soul

Most of us long for a soul mate, someone to whom we feel genuinely connected. We long to look into our lover's eyes and see the reflection of our worthiness and our perfection. Through love we hope to be given the keys to experience ourselves beyond our human limitations and flaws. We intuitively know that love can cast a spell over what is dull and ordinary and draw into being the beauty from the depths of our soul. The highest form of absolute love has an intelligence that bypasses our reason, control, and logic. This is the love the soul longs for, yet it is this love we also fear. This is the love that can turn our lives upside down and take us out of our controlled safety and into the open field of transformation.

We wish to attract a soul mate in part because we want to know our own soul more intimately. Within your desire for a soul mate is the longing to live more fully within the essence of your heart and your most loving and wise aspects. Yet the paradox is that until you become more conscious and aware of your soul, you cannot attract or sustain a relationship with a soul mate. The universal law of attraction states that *like attracts like*, and as you connect with your soul you will draw your soul mate to you.

Listening to the Soul

To perceive your soul is not easy. It is harder than paying attention to feelings, tuning in to body sensations, or noticing thoughts. The soul has been defined as the invisible life force of existence found in every living thing. It is self-aware essence: immortal, indestructible, and unique to each person.[2]

You cannot put your soul under a microscope and examine it. You can only know it through direct experience. As Ralph Waldo Emerson stated, "What we love is not in our will but above it. It is not you but your radiance. It is that which you know not in yourself and can never know."[3]

In your everyday life you can best know your soul through that which lifts your heart and makes your spirit sing. For me

---

2. June G. Bletzer, *The Encyclopedic Psychic Dictionary* (Lithia Springs, GA: New Leaf, 1998), p. 574.

3. Ralph Waldo Emerson, *Selected Writings of Emerson* (New York: Random House, 1950), p. 216.

this is a quiet walk along the river at dusk, or deep and honest sharing with a friend.

What you are drawn to, what your heart longs for, is your soul speaking to you. It is the constant reminder to let go of self-judgment, inner criticism, and negative self-talk. The flow of absolute love through the soul is a warm relief.

The soul is powerful. You know and feel this intuitively. Don't shy away from embracing your soul power. Its power lies in its connection with all that is; the soul does not have to seek out or compete for love and abundance. In those moments of heartfelt compassion and forgiveness, when you experience an expanded sense of unconditional love, joy, and oneness with all of life, you are in the presence of your soul. Your soul lives in love and when you surrender yourself to its influence and direction, you are guided to share this love with others.

The soul is your most powerful ally in manifesting all that you desire. It is, itself, creative freedom. As you become more able to live in the presence of your soul, you are more able to recognize the soulful presence of others.

Pamela

As I write this, I am interrupted by a knock at the door, and I am reminded that the soul speaks to us through synchronicity. It is Pamela, here for a session. We begin to talk, and within a few minutes she begins to cry. She tells me that she feels stuck in between her perception of herself as limited and powerless and her more recent revelation of herself as an empowered, creative being. Pamela tells me that everywhere she goes she hears the word *intention*, but she is reluctant to claim a conscious intention or a goal for her life. She says, as enticing as it may seem she is not ready for an inner paradigm shift. She feels as if her head is ready, in that she understands the potential that lies within her to create the life that she desires, but she feels overwhelmed and fearful of stepping into the unknown and a different way of doing things.

Pamela presupposes that listening to her inner voice and responding to life from a more soulful perspective means that she will be forced into having to do things that she doesn't feel competent or good at—those elusive things she knows are good for her but she doesn't do. When I press her to tell me what she thinks she would have to do, she tells me that she would probably have to stop making excuses as to why her business has never taken off financially. She would have to start to believe that she can attract a soul mate, and she would have to stop reading so many trashy novels. When I listen to her talk, I imagine that she fears the invisible soul police would be judging her decisions, ready to pounce on her if she does not adhere to soul rules like faith, trust, and hope. But the soul does not judge. It is absolute love and can never change or alter itself.

Soul Attraction

It is necessary to have a conscious relationship with your soul before you can have a relationship with a soul mate. This is because you cannot manifest what you do not know. If you long for a soul mate, it is because you long for a joy and connectedness that transcends the material-physical limitations. This is soul. Follow the impulses of joy, and you are on your soul path. Follow it long enough and your relationships will transform into soul relationships.

There is a magical alchemy of spirit that bypasses our rational reality. Like a bee drawn to a field of flowers, you attract that which best nurtures and loves you when you make choices in your daily life to enhance your connection to the soul. The love that you feel is the love you will attract.

How to Attract a Soul Mate

You can intuitively attract a soul mate by increasing your soul love vibration. The following activities are designed to create the most positive and attractive energy with which to draw you and a soul mate to one another. Use a journal to keep a record of each activity.

Strengthen Your Loving

Begin by generating love—easy, pleasurable, and gentle love. Put energy and action into your loving, especially love with no expectations. Listen to your heart. Discover what uplifts you, what makes you smile and laugh, what causes your heart to open, and what flushes your body with warmth. Love something passionately. Love your dog or cat; love nature, a tree in your yard; love art, music, dancing, architecture, travel, color, books; love a walk in the woods, the laughter of children, a beautiful sunset. Take time to stop and feel love flowing through you.

Take every opportunity to strengthen your loving. Love without expectation.

Write down in your journal the activities and occurrences when love moves you. You can also add pictures, poems, and photographs. Don't label some love as insignificant and some love as magnificent. The purpose of love is to love.

Heal Your Relationship Energy

Absolute love will respond to your request for a soul mate by bringing into your awareness any thoughts, beliefs, or emotional wounds that need to be released. You may also find yourself attracting potential partners that are anything but soul-mate material or you may find yourself in situations that provoke fear or self-judgment. Attracting difficult situations and relationships is the soul's way of getting your attention. If you find yourself attracting unsatisfying relationships or not attracting any relationships at all, go within and ask your inner guidance to help you to understand the meaning behind what is happening. Every situation or person that you attract is a direct reflection of what needs to be acknowledged and healed within you. You intuition can help you to get the message, heal, and move forward.

Forgive Others

Notice opportunities to practice forgiveness. If someone wrongs you or ignores you, regardless of who it is, consider it an opportunity to forgive, and do so without hesitation. The bigger the wound, the larger the wrong, the more positive energy you can generate by forgiveness. Forgiveness transforms negativity and creates a flow of available creative energy.

You may think that forgiveness leaves you vulnerable to being hurt again or that forgiveness discounts your suffering. Forgiveness, in fact, is an act of power. It instantly lifts you out of harm's way; it breaks your magnetism to pain.

In my own life, my father provided me with the lesson of forgiveness. He left our family when I was seven. I attended his wedding a few years later but saw little of him after that. I was born on my father's birthday, and every year I expected a birthday present or card from him. But it never came: no card, gift, or even a phone call. I wondered how he could so easily forget about me. The pain of this shadowed me. Nothing that I have ever done has changed this and believe me, I've tried.

Only forgiveness has allowed me to let go. It has placed me in the arms of love as a free soul. I cannot change my father, but forgiveness released me from the bondage of pain and negativity.

Break Free from Bondage
You might intuitively know that you need to forgive someone in order to move forward in love, but you are having a difficult time doing it. If so, close your eyes and imagine that you are chained to the person. There is a heavy chain around your neck that keeps you bound to him or her. You are unable to move forward into a lighter, more loving energy. In this image, see yourself with tremendous resolve and strength; you are able to break the chain and free yourself. Choose freedom; this is forgiveness.

Forgive Yourself

Forgive yourself for all of your clumsy attempts to love and care for yourself and others. Love is a journey marred by blunders and choices that may cause you to distrust yourself and your ability to be intimate with others. Release yourself from any guilt and shame that you harbor. Even if you do not completely believe it, affirm daily that you forgive yourself and you forgive all others. Eventually this intent will soften your self-judgment and you will be able to let go and forgive. Write in your journal what you may need to forgive yourself for, and then do it.

Gratitude

Recognize opportunities to practice gratitude. Interpret the events of your life as a series of masterfully orchestrated events that support you in your quest for love. Believe that the universe is responding to your desire for a soul mate by providing the conditions that will draw the perfect person to you. Even though you may not understand the divine workings behind all that happens, trust that what happens is in your highest good and be grateful. Pay special attention to what appear to be small or even inconsequential daily events. The soul works quietly. Record in your journal those things that you are grateful for.

Beauty

An often ignored attribute of the soul is beauty. This isn't beauty as defined by our cultural consciousness, but rather the sublime spiritual beauty inherent in all of life. It is the perception of perfection beyond physical form. Watch a sunrise. Feel the dew on your skin. See the sun peeking through the clouds. Perceive that behind the beauty of nature is the sublime beauty of the soul expressing itself in the physical world.

I was on my way home one late afternoon and had to stop at a railroad crossing for a very long train. As it slowly made its way through the intersection, I noticed a large patch of wild roses and other wild flowers growing close to the train tracks. The late-afternoon sun flitted through the overhead trees, and little spotlight sparkles illuminated several bees busy at work. The train roared by, but the bees continued their work, apparently unbothered. It was no longer an inconvenient wait on my way home. It was, instead, a moment of transcendent beauty.

Notice the beauty of your environment and of your soul. Sensitize yourself to those instances when kindness and gentleness stir within you. Pay attention to how your soul longs to open to love like a flower spreading its petals to the early-morning sun. Open your spiritual eyes to life's beauty and write down these instances in your journal.

Love in Action

Whatever you give energy to, expands. When you express love in the world, you will begin to see it in the world. To be loved you must give love. This seems obvious but, still, we're often reluctant to extend love unless we are guaranteed a positive outcome. To experience love and to attract your soul mate into your life you must put love into action. When love is pent up and unexpressed, it creates an energetic impasse. Put your love into action: volunteer, help a neighbor, devote yourself to a cause, pick up trash, listen to another's grief, or give your vacation days to an ill employee. Do something for others that has no return, do it simply to express your love. Then write in your journal about those times you give love for its own sake.

Listen Within

Allow your intuition to guide you. Take time each day to sit in quiet silence.

Close your eyes and begin to take long, deep breaths. Continue to breathe, and whenever the mind begins to wander and chatter, bring your attention back to your breath. As you breathe in relaxing breaths, notice the stillness that lies within you. Draw your attention into this quiet inner stillness.

Affirm that you are attracting your soul mate into your life. When your mind begins to wander, come back to this affirmation. If feelings of doubt or negativity surface, thank them for revealing themselves; then release these feelings through your exhale and inhale of absolute love.

Pay Attention to Synchronicity

Your intuition may surface through synchronicity, or meaningful coincidence, or dreams. Do not judge some intuitive messages as more significant than others.

You may, for instance, feel guided to eat lunch at a restaurant, feeling certain that you will meet someone special there. You follow through, eat lunch at the restaurant, but nothing happens. Your true love does not show up.

You may feel a strong message to pursue a relationship with someone, and it goes nowhere. While you may have a desired outcome in mind, your intuition will lead you to the experiences you need in order to know yourself better, to purify your intent and to test your resolve. Trusting and acting on your intuitive impulses strengthens your abilities. The more you follow your heart, the better you will become in understanding where you are being led and what you need to learn there. Following your intuition establishes you in the beautiful web of life and love's magical journey.

Be the Fool

Going back to our tarot deck, the 0 card is the Fool. The Fool represents spontaneity, folly, openness, and faith. In one (Rider-Waite) tarot deck, the Fool is illustrated as a young wanderer, his eyes focused in the sky, who appears to be about to step off a cliff. The Fool can either be the first card in the tarot deck or it can be the last, and can represent your beginning or your final destination. When you allow intuition to guide you in love, you can feel like the Fool. You may be guided to a love partner through circumstances that make no sense.

Claudia

I had not heard from Claudia in several years. She called me one October afternoon to tell me that after being single for many years, she was ready to commit to a long-term relationship with her soul mate. Within just a few months of making this decision, she moved from North Carolina to the Pacific Northwest. She told me that she had a dream that had spurred her on. In the dream she was sitting in a beautiful and spacious home but not her current home. From the window of this home, she saw a young girl she knew was her daughter and a man who she knew was her husband, happily playing in the yard. She woke up excited and flowing with love. She told me that she did not feel as if the home in her dream was in North Carolina. She felt that she would have to move out of the state to realize her dream.

Soon after having this dream, the state of Oregon kept surfacing, through odd coincidences. An old friend called her from Oregon. The main character in the book she was reading moved to Oregon. Her personal trainer had moved to North Carolina from Oregon. Claudia read these as intuitive signs. She told friends and family that she was moving to Oregon. Most of her family and some of her friends thought that this was the kookiest thing that they had ever heard. They had a hard time believing that Claudia would find her true love in Oregon. They argued to Claudia that she rarely dated, she had never lived outside of the South, and there was absolutely nothing that they could see that would guarantee that she would be happier and more lucky in love in Oregon.

Despite their protests, within six months Claudia had found a job and moved to Oregon. I heard from her about four months after she'd left North Carolina. She told me that shortly after starting her new job, she was asked to go to a large convention. While attempting to follow the complicated ramblings of one of the speakers, she locked eyes with a man who was sitting across the room. She told me that she instantly knew that he was the man that she had come to Oregon to meet. They were seated at the same table at lunch, and in polite conversation discovered many common interests. He volunteered to show her some pastoral nature trails the following weekend. Claudia told me that they have been hiking, talking, and enthusiastically getting to know one another, and that if she had any doubts about moving to Oregon, they are gone. She knows that she made the right decision.

Law of Action

Write down in your journal those times you listened to and acted on your intuition. Another universal law, *the law of mind-action*, states that in order to manifest what you desire, you must put into action the thoughts, feelings, and beliefs that support that desire. This universal law is also illustrated in the African proverb *When you pray, move your feet*. Commit to acting on your intuitive messages. If you wake one morning motivated to join a dating service or sign up for a conference, do it. If you feel led to start a conversation with a quiet co-worker or to attend a party that you might not normally go to, follow your intuition and act on it. Develop the ability to respond in positive ways to your intuition.

Calling In Your Soul Mate

The final part of this exercise is to open your heart and invite your soul mate into your life. You can attract your soul mate like a bee to a flower. Once you open the door to your heart, love cannot help but enter.

Read over your journal and enjoy the many instances of love, forgiveness, gratitude, beauty, and intuitive responses that you have documented. These instances of soul awareness can now act as money in the bank. They are valuable currency under the universal laws of *like attracts like* and the law of mind-action. Imagine that all of the energy you have invested in acts of soul recognition now acts as a powerful magnet that draws you and your soul mate to one another.

- Close your eyes and begin to breathe and relax, with each breath relaxing more and more. As you exhale you release any tension or stress you are holding in your body.

- Breathe into your heart, and feel it open and expand. Into your heart bring the forgiveness that you have offered. Recall the beauty that you witnessed and gratitude that you have chosen to express. Feel love flow through you. Listen to your inner, intuitive voice calling you into a quiet, heart-centered space where you feel empowered. Keep breathing into your heart, and feel the purity and strength of your soulful actions flow through you.

- When you are ready, invite the presence of your soul mate into your heart. Open your heart and experience the connection with your soul mate.

- Communicate with your soul mate that you are ready to receive his or her love and presence in the physical world. Imagine your soul mate by your side. Are you comfortable with their presence? Are you ready to share yourself and your life with another?

- Pay attention to any feelings of vulnerability or your tendency to guard your heart. Breathe through any tightness or fear. Keep inviting love into this space. Feel the safety of opening your heart and of loving.

- Ask for divine guidance about anything that will assist you in manifesting this soul-mate relationship. Guidance may come in as a feeling, an image, or an inner knowing. It may come as an emotional healing with feelings of love, warmth, and compassion. Pay attention and allow any guidance or information for your highest good to emerge.

Record your feelings and impressions in your journal. Daily practice of this meditation is the most powerful action you can take to attract your soul mate. Along with the meditation and other exercises, listen to your intuition. Act on subtle suggestions to go to certain places, events you might not normally attend, and follow up on synchronicities and seeming coincidences. Keep an open mind and an open heart. It has been my experience that the divine has a wonderful love journey planned for each one of us. Trust the divine to take you beyond your expectations and judgments.

Jill

Jill is a friend of my daughter. She very much wanted to be in a meaningful relationship. She brought her desire for a soul mate into her actions and meditations and opened her heart, inviting him in. One morning she excitedly called me to tell me about an uncanny coincidence.

Jill told me that for months while getting ready for work in the morning she would daydream about going back to school and studying literature. There was no practical reason to do this. Even though she enjoyed the classics and was an avid reader, she was busy in her career as a paralegal and would not have time to devote to class work, especially if it had nothing to do with her job. On her way to work one morning, she heard a radio ad about classes that were soon to start at a local college. She came home from work that evening, and in her mailbox she found a catalogue for the same college. She browsed through it and saw literature classes were being offered. One offering particularly interested Jill, and it was to be held in the evening. The next day, she enrolled.

At the first class meeting, Jill sat next to a pleasant man who had a warm smile. The first assignment was to select a book from the reading list and present to the class passages that illustrated the book's main theme. Jill went right to work and came to class prepared. The teacher asked for volunteers to present the assignment. The man sitting next to her raised his hand. He stood up and started to read from the same book that Jill had picked—not only the same book, but the exact passage she had chosen.

The theme of the book was unspoken love, and the passage spoke of two people who, although separated by unpreventable circumstances, share a deep love for one another.

Jill was surprised at the remarkable coincidence, and she volunteered to read her passage next. The man met her after class and asked her out for coffee to talk about the book they had both enjoyed. As they sat shyly looking into their coffee cups, they both realized a surprising familiarity and comfort level with one another. They each intuitively knew that they had discovered in one another a kindred spirit. They have been together ever since.

Recognize the Signs

When it comes to recognizing your soul mate, it is important to move beyond your intuitive type. When your attraction to another is focused only through your intuitive strength, you are likely to mistake a like-minded or similar individual for a soul mate. Soul mates do not always love us the way we want to be loved. Instead, they love us the way that we *need* to be loved, for our healing and soul growth and ultimate bliss. Soul mates often bring to one another differing perspectives, opposing viewpoints, and become a mirror for each other's strengths and weaknesses.

Recognizing a soul mate takes time and patience. To know if someone is your soul mate, check for these intuitive clues, especially the ones that are not your predominant intuitive type.

In the Presence of a Soul Mate

The physical intuitive will experience a soul mate through undeniable physical attraction and chemistry. They will likely feel intuitive soul-compatibility direction through surges of physical energy, and they may need less sleep, eat little, enjoy exercise, and have loads of physical stamina. They have the empowered belief that they are able to accomplish any task or goal.

The mental intuitive will feel what is called "peak" mental experiences. They will be able to spontaneously understand the meaning behind past perplexing situations and relationships. They will be able to see the big picture and have a sense that everything in life is just the way it is meant to be. Feelings of gratitude for past struggles and unsuccessful relationships will surface as they become aware that these conditions were necessary lessons on their path to their soul mate. Where once there was disharmony and emotional pain, there is now only understanding and acceptance.

The heart of the emotional intuitive will fully open, experiencing the full emotional spectrum of love. They will love not only their soul mate, but the disgruntled employee at the grocery store, the stranger who asks for a handout, or the relative who has always been difficult. Soul-mate love will inspire the emotional intuitive to love everyone and everything. Compassion, forgiveness, kindness, and the benevolence of the divine flows freely from them. They cannot contain their joy. The paradox of loving a soul mate is that the love becomes too big for just two people. It embraces the world.

A spiritual intuitive will experience the soul mate as wholeness, completion, and blissful rest. The soul relaxes and basks in the energy and light of its partner. The spiritual intuitive may have seen their soul mate in their dreams, or in a vision or meditation, and they are likely to have experiences of déjà vu with them. They will have an inner knowing that they have been predestined to meet this person and that they can now go about the business of fulfilling their soul purpose and mission in the physical world. Soul mates inspire one another to transcend self-absorbed focus and become a light of love for others.

Every Relationship Has a Purpose

Every relationship that you are in is important. Each one is an opportunity to heal and love. The universe supplies us with endless possibilities to experience love and connection. Even if you are not in a true soul-mate relationship, every person you encounter is preparing you for the ultimate experience of love.

Soul mates are never in short supply. It may be necessary that you interact with and love many people during your life. We sometimes forget that the soul learns through pain and disappointment as much as it does through the lofty feelings of happiness and joy. All we experience is food for the soul. Cherish your relationship misfortunes and disasters. They are the deep, rich-tilled, and composted soil that the seed of soul-mate love may need in order to grow, sprout, and come into full flower. Even when a relationship "fails," you do not have to.

Don't try to outguess the wisdom of love. Trust that there is a higher plan at work and a purpose for every relationship that you have been and will be in.

17

FUN AND GAMES
WITH INTUITIVE ROMANCE

~~~~~~~~~~~~~~~~~~~~~~~~~~~~~~~~~~~~~~~

We all share the same secret. We want to be known and appreciated, and submit to the power of love. Romance gently coaxes us to surrender and yield to love's warm current.

Intuitive awareness often unknowingly begins between two people during the initial getting-to-know-one-another period. When romantic feelings begin to stir, the intuitive connection grows even stronger. Romance has an instinctual and alluring aura, and in many ways it is intuitive. It is sensing and feeling what another feels, tuning in to their likes and dislikes, and creating an atmosphere of compatibility and sensuality. When romance and intuition consciously join forces, it stimulates and promotes deeper levels of confidence, trust, and mutual enjoyment.

Romancing by Intuitive Type

Each intuitive type will respond and be stimulated by somewhat different romantic gestures. When you know your partner's intuitive-love type, you can create a mood that will promote intimacy and trust. If you are not sure what your partner's intuitive type is, experiment with each one and pay attention to his or her reactions.

Physical Intuitives
Physical intuitives respond best to activity, touch, and physical connection. They will enjoy walking in nature, watching the sunset, sailing, bike riding, exploring the natural world, and any activity that they can actively participate in. To encourage closeness and increase intimacy with a physical-intuitive partner, offer to give him or her a foot message; hold hands; softly touch a shoulder, arm, or leg; and cook your partner a delicious meal. Physical intuitives are for the most part uncomplicated and easy to get along with. They are upfront and genuine, and they may not always understand love as a higher emotional/spiritual experience. For them love is physical, and they enjoy love energy in tangible forms like cuddling, passionate kisses, and lovemaking.

If you are romantically involved with a physical intuitive and want to know how he or she feels about you, listen and pay attention to how your partner talks about his or her physical health and well-being. If your partner has a lot of energy, is ready to participate in just about any activity, he or she is into you. If your partner is lackluster, tired, or needs to rest, move on.

To draw closer to a physical intuitive, send love energy through your touch and let the physical intuitive know that you enjoy being physically close to him or her.

Mental Intuitives

Mental intuitives are stimulated by conversation, ideas, and intrigue. They will open up when you ask them for their views on any topic. But keep it nonconfrontational and not overly intellectual; try topics like philosophy, mythology, ancient cultures, art, and the latest technology. Mental intuitives will respond positively and enthusiastically if you ask for their thoughts or help on personal or work-related issues or concerns. (Stay out of areas that are overly emotional.) They will like games, puzzles, the offbeat, the unknown, and the mysterious. Mental intuitives enjoy dates where they can learn and explore. This might mean attending a lecture or workshop on a topic of mutual interest, going to a Renaissance fair or a museum, or browsing a bookstore.

The mental intuitive in love will be able to intuit what is meaningful and important to you and will often go the extra mile to implement a plan to surprise and romance you. I have a friend who is a mental intuitive who planned a golf weekend for her hardworking husband. She knew that golf lessons would ease his stress and clear his mind. Without knowing anything about golf, she went about choosing an instructor, golf course, and weekend, all of which worked perfectly with his needs and schedule. When he asked her how she managed to get everything right, she just smiled and realized that her intuition had been spot on.

Spiritual Intuitives

Spiritual intuitives are sensitive creatures who respond to subtle cues in their environment. The physical intuitive tunes in to the concrete world of nature, activity, and touch, while the spiritual intuitive is instead attuned to color, light, sounds, smells, and the overall mood of the environment. They will enjoy soft-lit rooms, fragrant smells, and soothing music, as well as exciting environments like amusement parks, concerts, and the circus. They are drawn to the unplanned, the unusual, and they feel comfortable in a variety of settings. They may, for instance, enjoy both adrenaline thrills as well as the sublime atmosphere of quiet, calm peace.

To get the attention of a spiritual intuitive, ask him or her to help you interpret your dreams and discuss the possibilities of past lives, especially if he or she thinks that you had one together. Stimulate him or her with gentle light touch and soft whispers. Where the other types might find it odd or silly to silently look into one another's eyes and feel the "energy," the spiritual intuitive will be entranced. The key to the spiritual intuitive is exploring the abstract and elusive, and participating in spontaneous fun and magical adventures.

Emotional Intuitives

Emotional intuitives need and desire emotional experiences and they long to feel intense passion. They are in this world to explore emotion in all of its variety. For some emotional intuitives if a relationship is too calm or lacking robust exchanges, they may kick things up by becoming overly dramatic or even argumentative in order to feed their thirst for emotional energy. There is also the opposite kind of emotional intuitive who will steer away from conflict and emotional intensity at any cost. Because of their tendency to intuitively absorb the emotional energy of their environment, they will withdraw from too much excitement and seek out a tranquil and serene partnership.

Emotional intuitives will enjoy romantic and touching movies, strolling together hand and hand under the stars, and candlelit dinners. Give them flowers, small unexpected keepsake gifts, and of course let them know that you are saving mementos from your first date. They respond to acts of kindness, generosity, and most of all sharing your feelings of love.

Be emotionally genuine. An emotional intuitive will know if you are not. They will intuit your feelings with surprising ease, so don't be inauthentic and play games. If an emotional intuitive asks you how you feel, be honest. The interest in knowing is not to control, manipulate, or judge you. For an emotional intuitive, feelings are the real meat of partnership.

Tell him or her all about your misfortunes and your disappointments in love. An emotional intuitive will patiently listen and send you love from the soul to heal your wounds. A curious quality that many emotional intuitives share is that they are more likely to trust you if you share your hard times with them. This gives them the opportunity to open their heart and love you. They very much need to be needed.

The magic words emotional intuitives long to hear are "I love you." Without them they will become cold and distant, and with them they will open their heart and soul.

Partner to Partner

Not only can intuition help you to understand and romance your partner better, it also can be a fun and inspiring shared activity. Consciously embracing intuition in relationships strengthens both intimacy and the intuition-love connection. In my intuition development classes I find that in exercises that focus on individual intuitive self-awareness, students usually experience mediocre results. When we do partner exercises, however, the room comes to life, the psychic energy increases, and the outcomes become exciting. This is even more evident when intuition is focused in intimate relationships.

Partnership at its best is the attunement of two souls who become one in the soul of love. This kind of connection transcends physical and ego-based boundaries. Intuition can fine-tune the multidimensional connection that you share with the one who rocks your world.

Try these exercises:

- Look into your partner's eyes often and say, "You are beautiful." The eyes are the windows of the soul.

- Sit in the backyard or a place in nature in lounge chairs, or lie together on a blanket. Hold hands and stare up at the sky or the stars at night.

- If you suddenly think of your partner during the day, visualize a pink and white flow of love surrounding him or her.

- When you hold hands with your partner, send love and healing.

- Trust that your partner is a messenger from the divine, making an invaluable contribution to your life.

- Trust that divine forces have brought you into your partner's life for very important reasons.

- Have gratitude to the wise and loving power of absolute love for your partner.

- Believe that all the love and compassion you express to your partner will, in some way, be expressed back to you. Do not become attached to how or when it comes back to you.

- Take a silent walk in nature with your partner. Do not speak to one another for an agreed-upon time. Reach out energetically to your partner and embrace your connection with all of life.

- In meditation, ask your partner's spirit how you can best support their highest good.

- Remember that your partner has chosen to share his or her soul journey of love and relationship with you. Be patient and give your partner the benefit of the doubt. You do not fully know the particular challenges and past wounds that your partner has experienced. Know that your partner is doing the best that he or she can.

In times of disagreement, stress, or when you are feeling distant from your partner, try these exercises:

- *If your partner is a physical intuitive.* Participate in an activity together, especially one in nature—walking, hiking, bike riding, fishing, etc. Relax, breathe, and offer to give your partner a message. Using stimulating oils, listen to his body and establish an intuitive communication through your hands.

- *If your partner is an emotional intuitive:* Ask her to share her feelings, listen without advice-giving, play soothing music, and above all open your heart, as she will intuitively sense if your heart is open or closed. Express your feelings.

- *If your partner is a mental intuitive*: Give him space, do not push him to share his feelings. Instead, elicit ideas for improving communication and share your personal revelations and your perception of what is happening in the relationship. Be open minded and accepting of his reality. Meditate with one another on your shared purpose and the lessons that you are each learning through your relationship.

- *If your partner is a spiritual intuitive*: Allow her to be anxious and/or spacey and distracted. Get away from the television, cell phones, and computers (technology can further agitate a spiritual intuitive). Light scented candles, dim the lights or go outdoors, sit quietly with one another, and hold her hand. Tell a funny story; ask her what her guide and angels would say about your present relationship predicament.

Going Deeper with One Another

Intuition can guide you into the unspoken and uncharted inner territory of the soul. Being able to consciously tap into a power greater than your own can provide the necessary insight and guidance, thereby creating harmony and mutual understanding with your partner. Intuitive awareness can help you empathetically understand another, be sensitive to his or her needs and concerns, and know your own deep needs and desires. Intuition creates an energetic connection that fortifies the bond between two individuals. Two individuals sharing with one another from the depths of their soul create an eternal union that no outside influence can disrupt.

Joint Dreaming

One way to increase the intuitive energy between two people is to keep a joint dream journal. Sharing and documenting your dreams stimulates the unconscious flow of energy between you. It can provide you both valuable insight into yourselves, your partner, and aspects of the relationship that you may be unaware of. It gives the spirit of the relationship a means of expression as it spiritualizes and strengthens the soulmate connection.

It is not unusual with this practice to begin to have similar or even the same dreams. Pay attention to them and write down those dreams that seem to relate to your partner or to the relationship. You can also establish an intent before you go to sleep to have a dream that will shed light on a relationship issue. This could be a form of spiritual counseling. You and your partner might ask for divine guidance in the common areas of relationship concern, finances, communication, or sexual intimacy. Through interpreting and sharing your dreams with one another, new insights, fresh ideas, and a common unconscious language can be established.

Intuition-Focused Games

One of the most interesting and enjoyable aspects of intuition and intuitive development is the sudden and unexpected *Ah-ha!* feeling that comes when your intuitive impressions bear themselves out. When your extrasensory ability is on target, and you have correctly interpreted an intuitive impression, you can feel a rush of excitement and exhilaration. It is possible to experience the same kind of heightened intuitive discovery with a partner. A shared intuitive, energetic connection keeps a relationship fresh, and also infuses it with warm feelings of pleasure and elation.

Intuition-focused games are not only entertaining, they can also sharpen and increase intuitive aptitude; try these. Or make up your own!

- Buy a gift, wrap it, and then have your partner hold it and try to intuit what is inside. Your partner may sense the shape, color, and texture, or where or what it might be used for. Your partner can only open it once he or she has had a few accurate intuitive hits.

- On slips of paper, you and your partner write down love gestures—a kiss, hug, massage, foot rub. Then, write down some less-romantic activities like: cook dinner, fold laundry, go to the grocery store. Fold the papers and put them in a bowl. Taking turns, you will pick and intuit what it says. If you are correct, your partner (or you) has to do what is written on the paper.

- While driving on a stretch of road with little traffic, intuit the color, make, or model of the next car you see.

Explore variations of this: what will the next billboard be advertising, what color will it be, what numbers or shapes?

• Write down your fantasies on different pieces of paper. Be adventurous! Explore possible past-life scenarios. What was your relationship like in a different time and place, maybe even a different galaxy? Fold the papers and put them in a bowl. Have your partner pick one. While holding the paper and closing his or her eyes, your partner will tune in to what is written. If your partner correctly intuits a few aspects of your fantasy, you act it out together.

• Blindfold your partner. Have him lie down, and scan his body with your hands and then place your hand, for a few moments, over a part of his body. See if your partner can sense which part it is. If your partner is correct, you massage that area of his body.

• Have your partner comfortably lie down and close her eyes. Pass some essential oils under her nose without saying which ones you are using. Allow her to breathe deeply, taking in the scent. Give her a few moments to become sensitive to any part of her body, mind, or spirit that feels stimulated or energized. Use essential oils that stimulate intuition, psychic awareness, and sexual desire.

1. Jasmine increases optimism, joy, and harmony.
2. Sandalwood encourages intuition and psychic energy.

3. Coriander stimulates the hormones for increased sexual desire, and lavender enhances blood flow to the sexual organs.

4. Neroli is a powerful aphrodisiac that also reduces stress.

- Hide a piece of lingerie, a funny costume, or a silly mask somewhere in the house. Have your partner intuit where it is or in what part of the house you have hidden it in. Your partner has three tries; if he or she is correct, you must wear it.

- Imagine that you are a sex goddess or god and that you embody all the fine attributes of a gifted and giving sexual partner. Decorate your bedroom like a temple or shrine.

- While making love as a sex goddess or god, intuit where your partner's body is most sensitive to touch. Embody the attributes of a gifted, sensual, and intuitive romantic. Intuitively explore your lover's body, allowing it to communicate its desire for pleasure to you. Listen and respond.

Play with your intuition and make up your own games and interesting activities.

Even if your partner is not open to the idea of developing his or her intuition, experiencing is believing. One person's opening himself or herself to energy can bring forth unexpected and positive harmony and connection for both people.

18

IN THE BEDROOM: SEXUAL INTUITION

~~~~~~

Intuition describes the way that we relate to energy, and this includes sexual energy. Becoming conscious of your natural intuition can add a vibrant dimension to sexuality and love-making. Intuitive awareness sensitizes you to respond to your partner's whole being—mind, body, heart, and spirit. An intuitive connection with another infuses the relationship with excitement. It elevates lovemaking and stimulates peak sexual experiences. When your intuitive senses are awakened, you can listen and respond to the unspoken desires of your partner. Together, you can experience the pleasure of oneness.

Love's Unpredictable Ride

Sexual intimacy is an opportunity to experience heightened levels of connection with another and, simultaneously, with the divine. Sex can give us an energetic boost into the experience of the higher realms. The experience of orgasm can be a peek into the world of pure energy and bliss. It is like a sudden magic carpet ride into the ethereal.

Your sexual attraction to another is not always predictable and logical. It may even seem to be a force that is difficult to control and understand. While it might feel wonderful, it is sometimes overwhelming, as you may be fearful of opening yourself up to possible rejection or disappointment.

Sexual desire is a powerful force, and it can motivate us to move beyond our apprehensions and inspire more confidence in us than we knew we had.

Spiritualizing Sex

Unfortunately, lovemaking is not always a pure ride into mutual soulful paradise. Our ingrained beliefs and misconceptions about sex can increase our apprehension and fear. Sexuality is often darkened under the shadow of shame and guilt. Our culture has isolated sex from its spiritual core, and because of this it can become mechanical, habitual, and often unsatisfying. Although we all have the potential for satisfying sexually intimate experiences, we often engage in sex as a way to numb our spirit and emphasize our physical and material prowess. Or, we try to avoid it altogether.

Adriana and Terrence

Adriana, a bright and attractive twenty-five-year-old single client, met Terrence though an online dating site that focuses on people who have an interest in spirituality. They communicated through e-mails for about a week before they met for lunch.

Adriana and Terrence shared common beliefs about the nature of the universe and God, and they both had studied metaphysics.

At their first meeting, Adriana and Terrence each felt a surge of energy move through them, a pleasant warm tingling sensation. There was a natural chemistry and a mutual attraction. Even though it was their first meeting, the magnetism between them was so intense that they made love that evening. Their first sexual encounter was exhilarating, and Adriana felt more passion than she had ever felt. She could feel her body responding and opening to Terrence's physically powerful and robust sexual offerings. She felt as if she could soak in his masculine vibration, and as she did so she was elevated to new heights. Terrence was in the zone, like a deep meditative state. He experienced stimulating swells of energy move through him. Like the deep heavy currents of the ocean, he moved with rhythmic instinct.

Adriana and Terrence saw one another the following week and the week after. Each time they met their bodies responded by creating an environment of sexual pleasure. Their verbal communication was minimal, as they both felt a wordless connection to one another. They continued to see each other for many weeks.

Eventually, as much as Adriana looked forward to her dates with Terrence, she started to feel confused. As familiar as she was with him physically, she realized that she did not really know him. Terrence was pleasant and kind, and she wished to know him better. But each time they met, they found themselves wrapped in passion, with little conversation. In time, their already infrequent phone conversations dwindled even further, and their dates became fewer. One day they ran into each other at the grocery store. They both felt awkward and shy. Fumbling over the organic fruit when they locked eyes, they both knew that their relationship was over.

Amy and Jack

We can also resist the sexual love journey altogether. Sexual energy can often feel threatening and unsafe. The feeling of opening and merging with another can feel like too much of an emotional and spiritual risk. We may feel that we need to control ourselves and the life force in order to be safe. This is what happened in Amy's marriage.

Amy has been married to Jack for seventeen years. He is ten years older than Amy, and theirs was a second marriage for both of them. She met Jack a few years after her divorce while working at a nonprofit health clinic. She also worked long hours as a devoted volunteer community organizer. Jack was an elected official in the town where they both lived. He too was active, with a rich social life. He gave off the aura of confidence and security, which attracted Amy. She felt as if she could relax with Jack and that he would take care of her.

They saw one another about once a week for the first nine months of the relationship. They went to the movies and to dinner. Jack was attentive to Amy, always wanting to make her feel comfortable. He would gently kiss her at the end of their evenings together. There were no sexual overtures or passionate embraces. Amy appreciated Jack's calm nature, and she took it as a sign that he was a gentleman. She enjoyed the predictable rhythm of the relationship. Their attraction was based on their ability to comfort and emotionally support one another. Jack saw Amy as kind and attractive. He felt loved and appreciated by her.

They were married quietly by a justice of the peace ten months after meeting. Their marriage continued in the same peaceful and predictable manner, but, not surprisingly, their sexual relationship never quite got off the ground. Their sexual passion never ignited, and despite the many good qualities of their connection, Amy began to crave sexual intensity. Within the first year of the marriage Amy began to flirt with her male co-workers, and a year later she was having an affair with her boss. When I first met Amy she had been married to Jack for ten years. She had not had sex with him for seven of those years. Amy felt guilty about the many sexual encounters that she had outside of her marriage, yet she felt as if she still loved Jack and was not ready to divorce him.

Love Is a Circuit Board

Sexual energy is a vital part of a healthy body, mind, and spirit. It is also an important part of your relationship with a beloved partner. Your energy body is like a circuit board of flowing vibration. Adriana and Terrence were primarily connecting through sexual energy. Through their lovemaking, they were able to experience heightened states of awareness and connection. Unfortunately, they did not have the kind of heart connection necessary for a relationship to thrive. The passion soon fizzled. In contrast, Amy and Jack shared kindness and love for one another, but their relationship did not have much juice.

It lacked energy and stimulation. They got along just fine, but there was no glue to hold them together. For intimate relationships to thrive, it is necessary that essential and life-affirming energy flow through both partners.

The Full Experience

To reap the rich bounty of spiritual lovemaking, it is necessary to open yourself—mind, body, heart, and spirit—to the power of love. To set the stage for an enlightened sexual encounter it is necessary to broaden one's intent and focus. When lovemaking is a physical and an emotional and spiritual heart-opening experience, true intimacy and connectedness is possible. Longing and desire for personal satisfaction can be replaced with attentiveness and generosity toward your partner. Instead of the self-centered view of having your needs met through another, you can surrender to the moment and wholly merge with your partner.

Complete Sexual Intimacy

Each intuitive type is especially tuned in to a specific aspect of lovemaking. Physical intuitives are comfortable with sexual energy. They are able to encourage and generate intense sexual sensations throughout the body. At their most developed they can sensitize the body to receive the higher vibration currents of absolute love.

The mental intuitive brings to lovemaking the gift of mindfulness and the ability to be calmly centered in present-time awareness. Instead of thinking about what to make for dinner or being distracted by a stressful day, at their most developed, mental intuitives can attune themselves to their partner's energy consciousness in attentive, rapt awareness. The emotional intuitive brings into lovemaking the open, expanded, vulnerable, and boundless heart. They can immerse themselves in the universal flow of absolute love and experience the divine beloved through their mate. Spiritual intuitives thrive on the sensations of ethereal, unseen, and supernatural energy. In the act of lovemaking they invite the presence of wordless, mystical passion. Ecstasy, excitement, visions of light and color are all part of their sexual experience.

When each of the four intuitive-love types is activated and developed within an individual, lovemaking can be a wild ride into the heavens.

Become It All

You can use the natural strengths of all of the intuitive types to improve and revitalize your lovemaking experience.

Try this: Find a time when you and your partner can be alone and undisturbed. Create a soothing and relaxing mood through music, soft lighting, and perhaps a soothing fragrant scent.

Use the energy of the mental intuitive to come into present-time awareness. Breathe and relax. Notice any tension in your body and continue to breathe and exhale any stress, thoughts, or concerns. Communicate with your partner, be completely present to her. Ask her about her day, her feelings, tell a joke, and most of all listen to her fully and attentively.

Soften your gaze, and begin to touch and lightly kiss your partner. Notice how you feel, what you sense, and keep bringing your awareness back to present time. Tune in to your partner and slip into a calm and relaxed, attentive mood.

Become aware of your body filling with increased sensation. Become the physical intuitive and feel sexual energy move through your body. Sexual energy is most often first experienced in the genital area. Breathe, feel, and move this energy up the spine. Extend this energy through touch and sensitivity to your partner's body. Your sexual energy empowers you and helps you to feel strong and capable of sexually pleasing another.

As the energy moves up the spine, allow it to collect in the heart. Inhale love and exhale it through the heart. Call forth the emotional intuitive inside of you and feel this energy as love. Open your heart and imagine waves of love energy caressing your partner. Allow your heart to open, breathe, and invite more energy into your body, mind, and spirit.

As your heart opens, tune in to sensation and vibration like the spiritual intuitive. Imagine an aura of intense color and light completely surrounding the both of you. Your lovemaking is opening a door to know yourself and your partner in new ways. You do not need words to describe this experience—just become love, become sensation, and trust the force and power of love to move through you and take you to elevated states of ecstatic union with the greater whole.

Flow with the energy of the different intuitive types, merging the energy of each within you. Move this intuitive sexual passion through you and share it freely with your partner.

Absolute Love Brings Forth Changes

The energy of love and intimacy between two people brings with it the possibility of altered states of awareness. When absolute love flows through your heart, you experience it as unconditional warmth, compassion, and bliss. Your mind experiences absolute love energy as higher states of awareness, consciousness expansion, and enlightenment. The body can experience this flow of absolute love energy through elevated states of ecstasy and orgasm, when the cells of the body literally vibrate at a higher rate. This can create a feeling of fluidity that can lead to the transformative sensation of your body's moving from a state of density to lightness and energy.

Curtis

My friend Curtis, an accomplished jazz musician, told me of a particular evening with his partner, Gisele, while they were vacationing in San Francisco. They had spent the day visiting art galleries and eating exotic food. That night while making love on a king-size bed in their small hotel room, Curtis looked into Gisele's eyes and saw the universe open within them. He felt the vastness of cosmic space while fiery warmth shot through his body. He knew then, as a golden light spread over them, that Gisele had traveled through the stars, through all of space to be with him. He knew that their love transcended all that had been and all that would ever be. He rested in this bliss as he now knew the power of love.

There are powerful forces at work during lovemaking. It is an opportunity to experience, integrate, and become one with a much grander life force than we under normal circumstances can know. Take advantage of this gift and allow the intuition-love connection to further unite you with your partner and to the soul of love in its most ecstatic dance.

PART IV

Real Help from the
Ethereal Realm

19

DEATH IS NOT THE END: RELATING TO LOVED ONES ON THE OTHER SIDE

O pen to and receive the love of the nonphysical realms. Many people are learning the lesson of love without form. It is not always easy to feel the presence of love when you are alone. When a loved one dies, the sting of loneliness can be particularly strong. During those times when we feel most alone, our understanding of what love is, is forced to evolve.

Love does not rely on form; love doesn't need a physical body through which to express itself. Although you know this intellectually, you may still suffer when the object of your love is no longer physically present. Intuitive ability offers you an avenue with which to increase your awareness that you are loved, even when no one is present. Through a conscious connection with the unseen, you are able to experience love in myriad ways.

Loved Ones in Spirit

Many people visit mediums (psychics who can communicate with people who have passed over) because they miss their loved ones after their death. Most people want to know that their loved ones are still present with them in some way, and they desire tangible signs to confirm their continued existence beyond physical form.

A bond of love between two individuals transcends the limitations of death. From the beyond, our loved ones are still very much alive in spirit. They long for us to feel their presence and know of their continued devotion.

Katrina

Katrina was a skeptic, who came to me to see if I could communicate with her deceased husband. Almost immediately, her husband, who had died many years before, came into our session, giving all kinds of advice and support for Katrina. Upon hearing the advice that I relayed from her husband, Katrina stopped me cold, stared into my eyes, and asked me to prove that it really was her husband.

I offered the challenge to Katrina's husband in spirit. He quickly took the opportunity to tell me that Katrina should stop being so cheap and get a new kitchen floor. He told me that Katrina had a broken tile near the stove and she just wanted to replace that one tile. Although Katrina's husband communicated to me through images and thoughts, the message came through loud and clear. Katrina was amazed that her husband could be so close. She told me that just that morning a repairman had come look at her kitchen floor, and her husband was correct; she was trying, unsuccessfully, to find someone to replace just that one tile.

Help from Beyond

Now in spirit and immersed in love, your loved ones can often help you in unexpected ways.

When my friend Rhea's mother was dying of colon cancer, she made a promise of specific help to each of her four children. Just a week before her death, she told Rhea that once she was in heaven, she would help her find someone who would love and adore her. Two years to the day after her mother died, Rhea sat across the table from Jeff, a handsome carpenter. They were set up by mutual friends, and although this was their first meeting, they felt as if they had known each other for a long time. Two years later they were married.

Your loved ones are usually more present than you would suspect. It may sound like a contradiction, but the reason it's hard to detect your loved ones' presence is because they are so close that you are used to their being around. How's that? Think about the music you hear at the shopping mall. When you first arrive, it seems so loud that you can hardly hear yourself think. By the time you are ready to leave, you barely hear the music. You have redirected your focus from the loud music to your shopping. So it is with your loved ones. You may, at times, perceive their presence, but mostly your attention is on the physical realm.

Intuitive-Love Types in Spirit

Each intuitive-love type is likely to make contact with loved ones in spirit in distinct ways. But be open to connecting with your loved one in a variety of ways. An interesting phenomenon that often happens when connecting with loved ones in spirit is that you are likely to experience their presence through their predominant intuitive type. For instance, if your loved one was a mental intuitive, she is likely to contact you through her thoughts and ideas.

Feeling the Love
Emotional intuitives are most comfortable with emotional energy. They are likely to come through as spontaneous feelings of warmth, comfort, and love. You may experience them as a surge of love that opens your heart and tangible feelings of calm reassurance. At times, their emotional presence will be so evident that tears are likely to well up in your eyes.

Crystal's husband, Brent, died of a heart attack several years ago. He was playing racquetball with a friend one Monday morning, just as they had for the past eight years. During a vigorous exchange he hit the ball, turned to look at his friend, and collapsed. Crystal got the call while driving their ten-year-old daughter to school. Brent died before reaching the hospital.

Faced with limited finances and mounting debt from a recent home remodeling, Crystal knew that she had to enter the workforce. She was nervous and anxious, and questioned her ability to find a decent job and take care of her family. One morning while sitting at the kitchen table, drinking coffee and feeling overwhelmed with grief, she felt what she called a warm breeze of love and comfort slowly creeping over her. She felt Brent's love merge into her heart, and she felt his gentle humor and stable presence assure her that everything would work out. With his warmth and strength from the other side, she had a renewed confidence that she could carry on.

The Presence of Helpful Wisdom
The mental intuitive will use ideas, memories, thoughts, and telepathy to communicate with loved ones. Have you ever driven down the highway or been engaged in a mundane task, and felt the uncanny presence of a loved one giving you advice or trying to help you figure out a problem?

My uncle Bob was an aeronautic engineer, and a very good one. Among his many projects, he was one of the main engineers of the original space shuttle. I remember him sitting in my car one evening, listening to it run for just a minute and then quickly diagnosing my engine problems. When I was in college struggling through mandatory math classes, I was often confused, lost, and generally not getting it. Luckily for me, my uncle stepped in and saved me more than once. Although he had died just a few months previously, I would often feel his calm and analytical presence guiding me through the maze of numbers and equations. When it comes to anything that is logical and precision oriented, I call on him for help.

When connecting to a loved one through the mental-intuitive avenue, it is likely that you will have difficulty distinguishing a loved one's thoughts and ideas from your own. To let you know of their presence, loved ones will often send you a message through your inner hearing. Have you ever turned around after hearing your name called and there is no one there, or have you heard a repeating verse of a song constantly replaying through your mind, or perhaps a voice that keeps telling you over and over to take some action? If so, pay attention. Someone is trying to get your attention.

A client told me that during a phone call to her daughter, loud static interrupted the conversation. In the static, she heard a male voice say, "You are loved." This woman said she knew it was her father, who had passed over a few months before, speaking to her.

Seeing Is Believing
Spiritual intuitives are the most likely to connect with loved ones though more ethereal and celestial experiences, such as seeing them as an apparition, a flash of color or light, or sensing their presence.

Dreams, another spiritual-intuitive means of expression, may be one of the most recognizable ways that loved ones make their presence known.

People often look for the presence of their loved ones in dreams, and are disappointed if they do not make contact in this way. Keep in mind that loved ones may not appear in dreams as the physical person that you remember. They may instead come through as a feeling of warmth and gentleness, a bird or other animal, or as a guiding but unrecognizable force.

Olivia

Olivia is in her mid-thirties, single, and very much wants a long-term, loving relationship. She told me of a dream she had about her father. He had taken her by the hand and led her to the downtown area of the city, where large white tents lined the streets. Hand in hand, they moved through the busy streets until they came to a narrow side street. Her father looked at her with a mischievous, warm smile and then disappeared. Olivia woke up and wrote down the details, then tried to decipher the dream's symbolic meaning. She came up with a number of possible meanings, none of which felt right.

A month or so later she accompanied a group of friends to the annual downtown art fair. Large white tents lined the streets, under which artists displayed their work, vendors prepared exotic food, and musicians warmed up for their performances. As Olivia wandered up and down the streets, taking in the colors, sounds, and interesting art, she noticed a remarkable display of wood carvings. She was fascinated by the rugged-looking artist, whittling a small piece of wood. She watched his strong hands create a small, angelic figure from a block of wood. They began to chat, and Olivia learned that his name was Erving and he lived a few hours away, in the mountains. They talked on, for what turned out to be an hour. Erving asked her if she would meet him after the fair ended to have dinner. Without hesitation, Olivia said yes.

Olivia didn't think of her dream until after she and Erving had dated for several months. She realized then that the dream was not a metaphor. It was really her father leading her toward Erving.

Tangible Presence

A physical intuitive is most likely to break through the material-world veil with physical manifestations. This might come in the form of the lights in your home flickering off and on, the television mysteriously changing channels, your clock stopping, or the doorbell ringing when no one is there. You might smell the familiar scent of a perfume, a favorite food, or flowers. Your loved ones may inspire a butterfly, bird, cloud, or stray animal to announce its presence.

You may feel the physical intuitive's presence most tangibly while sitting in his favorite chair or participating in an activity that he loved.

Justine's husband, George, had a passion for the ocean and deep-sea fishing. At least once a month, he could be found on the back of a fishing boat with a reel in one hand and a beer in the other. Just a few weeks before George passed over from lung cancer, he spent what he called a weekend in heaven, fishing with friends.

Justine never shared George's love of fishing—that is, until after he passed over, and she joined some of their mutual friends for a weekend at the coast.

Justine agreed to join these friends on a fishing trip and found herself early one Sunday morning sitting in the back of their rather plush boat. Watching the sun rise and mesmerized by the tranquil green-blue current, she suddenly and with undeniable clarity felt George sitting next to her. Tears came to her eyes as she smelled his familiar aftershave, and recalled his love of the ocean. She felt that he was telling her that he was at peace, and in return she let him know that she was finally getting "it." She, too, was now able to appreciate the tranquility that the ocean offered.

Spirit Island

The following meditation can help increase your intuitive connection with your loved ones in spirit. Practicing this meditation at the same time of day and in the same place will increase its effectiveness. To further reinforce the intuitive climate, use the same imagery each time you attempt to connect with a certain loved one. Establishing these kinds of patterns builds psychic energy and makes it easier for two souls to connect.

- Begin by choosing a quiet place where you will not be disturbed. If you have a picture or a personal item of your loved one, bring it into this space with you. Lie or sit down in a comfortable position. Close your eyes and bring your attention to your breath. Breathe in long, deep, relaxing breaths and exhale, releasing any stress and tension. Continue breathing and relaxing.

- As you continue to breathe, imagine walking along a seashore or the shore of a great river. You hear the rhythmic sound of the waves as they gently touch the shore. You feel a slight breeze and warm sunlight caressing your face, and you hear the sound of birds calling in the distance. The beauty of this place inspires you to feel love, peace, serenity, and tranquility.

- As you continue your walk along the shore, you are enveloped in a warm, white mist. As the mist begins to lift, you see a figure of luminous light coming toward you. You invite this radiant light to come closer, and as it does so it is somehow comfortingly familiar.

- On the shore you notice a small but sturdy boat. You climb inside and immediately feel safe and relaxed. This luminous bright light is close by and gets into the boat with you. You take the oars and steer the boat out into the water.

- You quickly make your way into the open water. As your boat glides along with the strong current, you notice what appears to be a landmass in the distance. As you draw closer to it, you observe that it is a lush and beautiful island.

- As you make your way toward the island, you notice that many people are standing along the shore. They are waving to you, and as you draw closer you begin to recognize them. These are your loved ones—family members and friends no longer living in the physical realm. They have passed into spirit and are excited to connect with you.

- You steer the boat onto the island, and you go to greet your loved ones.

- Spend a few moments in their presence, greet them, see them, listen to them, and accept their love and warmth.

- Continue to receive any impressions through thought, emotion, or sensation. A loved one may have something for you. It could be an object or symbol that does not make sense to you. Just accept whatever is offered without trying to figure it out.

- The brilliant light that has led you to this island now leads you back toward the boat. It is time to leave. Express your joy and gratitude to your loved ones for coming to meet you, and get back on the boat.

- You quickly and easily make your way back to the shore where you began. The warm light that has accompanied you recedes, and now merges back into the white fog.

- When you are ready, open your eyes and write down any impressions, feelings, sensations, or thoughts you experienced.

In addition to doing this exercise, pay particular attention to any signs of your loved ones' presence in your everyday life. Know that they are hard at work, attempting to make their presence known to you and to assure you of their love and well-being. Keep an open mind and heart about how your loved ones may break through, and never underestimate the positive influence they can have on your life.

20

LOVE LIKE THE ANGELS

~~~~~~~~~~~~~~~~~~~~~~~~~~~~~~~~~~~~~

Relationships are very human affairs. They can be messy, full of lust, and bring out the best and worst in us. Hardly the place, it seems, for a presence as pure as the angels. Angels are radiant aspects of love. In comparison, the love that we humans share and engage in can feel anything but innocent. Yet angels help us in our love relationships in ways that we do not suspect and cannot always detect.

Angels are truly the emissaries of love. When we desire and wish for the exalted soulful love of a generous and devoted partner, we are in angelic territory. This is the love that they wish for us to give and receive with one another. In the excited look in your lover's eye is the smile of an angel. Angels sneak into your vulnerabilities and fears, and encourage you to love more fully and deeply. Through times of despair and loneliness they are constantly beside you, easing your way. You might say that human relationships are their playground, where they delight in watching our triumphs and picking us up after our fumbles.

There is no place, time, space, or realm that an angel cannot access; the angelic realm is all-encompassing. Angels transmit unconditional love in waves of understanding and comfort, always offering compassion. Developing a conscious relationship with angels strengthens your ability to give and receive love in the human world.

How Angels Communicate

Angels work through your emotional and spiritual energy. When you open to their influence, they align with your emotional energy, offering support and healing. You may receive guidance and angelic messages in intuitive meditation and contemplation through visual impressions, images, color, and light, which is called *clairvoyance*. You may intuit angelic messages through *clairaudience*, which is the ability to hear words, songs, or phrases, and through *clairsentience*, which is the ability to sense their presence or feel a tingling sensation on or in your body.

You may not know when your angels are close. You might feel them as warmth, a sense of well-being, or a soft, expanded heart. At times you may sense a tangible yet invisible presence watching over you. We may not be able to put a name to it or identify who or what it is. It can be difficult for us to grasp and believe things that don't have names or form.

Conscious encounters with your angels often occur when you dream at night, in times of stress or trauma, or when you have asked for the angels' help and are open to divine synchronicity—that meaningful coincidence with an inner message.

Talk to Your Angels

The more you consciously engage your angels, the more they will guide and assist you. It is not weakness to ask for their help. It is instead an invitation for divine love to flow into your life.

My angels tend to be pretty busy, keeping me on relationship course. They are interestingly not as naïve about human nature as I am. I have the tendency to see the best, most positive aspects of others and will unfortunately disregard character traits and intuitive information that I should be paying attention to.

I remember one time when I saw, through the window of a bookstore, the familiar face of an intriguing individual whom I had recently met. I thought I would go in and say hello. As I opened the door to enter, it felt like I walked into a brick wall. There was a tremendous force of pressure pushing me in the opposite direction. I was taken aback and instead of going in, I turned around and sat on a bench. I heard the familiar inner voice of an angel imploring me to think about what I was doing. As I sat there I realized that maybe I was walking into something that was not good for me. (It wouldn't have been be the first time.) I trusted the message and went on my way.

This is usually how it works. You will receive a message like I did, which goes contrary to what you want and without factual evidence to back it up. The more time you spend connecting with your angels, the more confident you will be when given what feels like a contrary message.

Guardian Angel

You have a guardian angel that is devoted to you during the course of your lifetime. Your angel is always watching out for you through all of your ups and downs, encouraging you to love without reservation and hesitation. Guardian angels are especially pleased when you sense their presence.

Darien

Darien is an interesting man who has had a lifelong interest in metaphysics. His presence in my intuition-development class is always friendly and encouraging to others. Despite having had a harsh and distant mother as a child, he emits a feeling of heartfelt warmth. When Darien was ten years old, his father left his family of five. Darien remembers his mother working hard day and night, struggling to support her children. To help out, Darien started working at age twelve, delivering papers in the early-morning hours.

Darien married his high school sweetheart when he was just eighteen. The marriage lasted less than two years, and since that time he has dated only occasionally. Darien told me that sometimes as he is driving in his car, he feels a soft and loving feminine presence close to him. He also has dreams in which he feels the presence of the same warm and loving feminine spirit. Darien came to see me, wondering if the feminine energy that he had been sensing was a premonition of a woman that he is soon to meet.

Although Darien longs to be in a soul-mate relationship, the presence that he is feeling is his guardian angel, Tara. He seemed disappointed when I told him this, and I could not blame him. She is loving and devoted to him. She has his highest good as her focus. Their relationship is real and tangible, even though he is in body and she is in spirit. Tara is, in many ways, the closest and most loving companion Darien has. She is with him to help him feel the love he was denied as a child and to help him heal. As he becomes more accustomed to her presence, he will be more able to attract this same kind of love into his physical life.

Higher Vibrations of Empathy

Angels are highly empathetic in that they feel and sense what you are experiencing, and they are aware of the impact that it has on you. They seek to help you to let go of patterns of behaviors and beliefs that keep you from experiencing the kind of love that you truly deserve. Angels do not, however, take on your pain and suffering. They instead offer healing and relief from your burdens and worries.

In the human world, you may tend to absorb the emotions and stresses of other. You may do this unconsciously, believing that you can lighten another's burden. Unfortunately, carrying someone else's pain or stress does not help them or you. You simply become weighed down and weary. Angels can discharge negativity into the pure streams of transformative divine energy. You need only ask for their help; they will always respond to a request for healing. When you align your empathy with that of angels, you will be able to love others, feel their pain, and then release it to a higher love. When you do, you will feel an inner uplifting and lightness, and those with whom you have relationships will experience it, too.

Many people block their intuitive ability because they are highly empathetic, and the energy they absorb from others becomes overwhelming. The best way to avoid this is to love like the angels and ask to become channels for a higher wisdom and love. When your intuitive awareness is connected to the source of divine love, then your energy field is infused with healing vibrations that benefit everyone.

Attuning to Angelic Energy

When you consistently attune to the higher vibrations of the angelic realms, your aura or energy field in this heightened state becomes more luminous and resilient. Your aura is protected from psychic attacks, vampires, energy attachments, and environmental toxins. Simply ask for the angels' love and protection. Like a raindrop falling into the ocean, when we open ourselves to the will of a higher source we become one with the grand flow of love.

Angelic-Intervention Meditation

This intuitive meditation can be used to heal any relationship, especially if you are at a loss as to how to have more positive interactions. It can be used in any relationship in which you wish to feel more love, acceptance, and peace.

Begin by focusing on a present or past relationship that feels unresolved, confusing, or one that may continue to cause you stress. Write down the person's name and any thoughts or feelings that you associate with him or her. When you feel ready, proceed with the following meditation.

1. Find a comfortable position; you may want to lie down for this exercise. Close your eyes and take a long, deep breath, then exhale. Continue to breathe in, sending the warm energy of the breath to any part of your body that is sore or tense or tight. Then breathe out all of the tension or stress. Continue with this cleansing breathing; each time you breathe, draw in warm, relaxing white light and exhale any tension from the body.

2. Continue to breathe, and imagine a place in nature that is warm and inviting. You can feel and sense trees, flowers, and vegetation gently swaying to a slight breeze. You may hear water from a stream, river, or waterfall flowing in the distance. Perhaps you can also hear the sounds of birds chirping overhead. The sun is shining down on you, helping you to feel even more relaxed. The warm sunshine stands for all that is positive in life like love, kindness, and compassion.

3. This place in nature is a place of absolute love. All that is here is an expression of love. The flowers, the gentle breeze, and the soft sounds of water in the background are all vibrating in the essence of love. You can breathe in the absolute love surrounding you. It fills you with a delicious fragrance, it is satisfying and nurturing. Accept as much love as you can. Notice any blocks or stress in your body that may not be allowing love in. Breathe into this place, release the stress, and ask for the presence of love

to fill you. You will feel the presence of love surrounding you. Invite your angels to draw close to you, and continue to breathe in love.

4. Ask for the person's energy to come into this meditative space with you. Ask his or her spirit for an opportunity to bring healing to the both of you.

5. Your person may or may not want to enter. Allow your person to do as he or she wishes. Try to hold unconditional love with no expectations. Your person can find peace and serenity here. If your person is hesitant, send him or her the message that this is a healing place; there are no strings attached. Let go, and allow your angels and the energy of love to attend to him or her.

6. Intend for your relationship with your person to be healed by love. Allow the energy of love to initiate the healing. You must let go of your desired outcome. Ask your angels for their healing love and support.

7. Quietly listen and receive whatever message your person may have for you. What do you need to know or feel to be in a place of peace? Commit to whatever action, thought, healing, or forgiveness is asked of you. Allow the relationship to be healed. Send forgiveness, love, and acceptance to your person. Even if he or she has chosen not to enter your place of love, you can still send love—love with no expectations.

8. Stay in this energy for as long as possible, quieting yourself and listening to whatever comes to you. Thank your angels for their help. When you are ready, open

your eyes and write down in your journal any thoughts, feelings, images, or messages that you experienced.

Often, the impressions that you receive during meditation do not make sense at first, but do not disregard anything as unimportant. It may take days, or weeks, before you are able to comprehend the full meaning behind what seemed like random images, feelings, or impressions. Once you know something, there's the risk the ego-mind might minimize or sabotage its effect on healing. For this reason, deep healing happens apart from the logical, thinking mind.

You might draw or sketch the place you visited in this meditation. Creative activity can further stimulate intuitive receptivity. It is a good way to retain the energy of an experience without overanalyzing it.

You can come back to this place as often as you would like. Each time you do, additional healing will take place. Be aware that the healing is rarely obvious right away. It may occur on the physical, mental, emotional, or spiritual level, and it will, no doubt, take time for the healing to manifest in the physical realm.

21

SPIRIT GUIDES: A CONSTANT SOURCE OF POSITIVE ENERGY

Strengthen your relationship with your invisible, and often unknown, spirit friends. Not only do you have loving and devoted angels and loved ones in spirit, you also have spirit guides. Spirit guides are enlightened consciousness. They are especially adept at understanding and advising us in our most mundane and human situations and endeavors. This is because unlike angels, spirit guides have at one time inhabited our world as human beings.

Whether your desire is to attract a soul mate or revitalize a current relationship, know that when you invoke help from a spirit guide you are engaging powerful forces of positive energy.

Why Do They Help Us?

You may wonder why a soul immersed in the realms of love and perfection would want to help and assist you. We sometimes feel so small and insignificant when we compare ourselves to the wisdom and divine beauty of the heavens. Yet you too, at the core of your being, are a spark of divine love. Your spirit guides want to help you to remember this.

Spirit guides often continue to grow and evolve as we do. Their interactions with us help them to further their higher purpose of learning how to enlighten, love, and be of service to others. They are attracted to people who have similar challenges to ones they have encountered. They are drawn to you through your devotion and commitment to growth and transformation. These nonphysical friends and companions can help you understand and release the dusty old patterns of loving that no longer serve your highest good. They exist in the oneness of all of life and retain perfected individuality.

Guides Are Positive Energy

You might think that investing in ethereal connections is a waste of time and even a bit kooky. Yet when you view your life through an intuitive lens, it becomes increasingly clear that you are not just blood and bones but spirit and energy as well.

Spirit guides can influence your day-to-day affairs because they reside within the current of absolute love energy. Every relationship issue that you confront has been created by the energy of your thoughts, feelings, and beliefs. When you consciously allow your spirit guides into your life, you are injected with pure, positive energy. You can draw from this love energy to create more of what you want in your life and eliminate those things that have been created from negativity and fear. Even when you do not have direct evidence of the existence of your spirit guides, investing a bit of your time and attention to opening yourself to their influence can yield surprisingly positive results.

Communicating with Higher Energies

Communicating with spirit guides often begins with a leap of faith that they actually exist. It would be certainly more comfortable if our guides gave us their names and communicated their information in clear and obvious ways. In truth, their means of communication are usually more playful, surprising, and not always what we would expect them to be. It may be that your initial interactions are through synchronicities, meaningful coincidences.

One of the ways that my guides get my undivided attention is with the number 7. When that number shows up repeatedly in my accounts, the mileage on my car, or glances at the clock or phone numbers, I pay special attention to intuitive guidance.

You might hear your spirit guides as a quiet voice in your head that gives you insight or an original idea. They will motivate your growth and evolution in ways that do not always make sense at the time. This is especially true when it comes to relationships. While you might desire to attract a partner based on their outward characteristics, your spirit guides will instead steer you toward the individual who can offer you essential lessons about love.

Keep in mind that when it comes to love and relationships, your guide's agenda and your own may differ. My spirit guides are more interested in teaching me how to integrate absolute love into my life and cultivate the ability to attract a partner than they are in simply putting the "right one" at my doorstep. They have not shielded me and saved me from the lessons that I have needed to learn about myself and love.

I remember asking them once when a relationship ended, why they didn't warn me and make the outcome clearer before I got involved. In response I felt their calm presence telling me that there are certain souls that have helped me to reclaim parts of myself, and even though the relationship did not go down the path of happily ever after, it was not in vain. They know that as long as I look for love and happiness from another, I am not embracing the truth of love. At the time, I would have just as well skipped the lesson, but I know that the conscious path of absolute love is not a pass-or-fail test. It is instead an adventure where all that comes your way, each person, and each situation—despite the outcome—will bring you into the heart of absolute love.

Laura and Rob

Spirit guides often create situations and circumstances in your everyday life that will help you to grow and accept your highest potential. They don't allow us to settle into relationships that merely skim the outer edges of love. Even when we are comfortable with just a smidgen of love, they are not. This is what happened to Laura.

I have known Laura, a hard-working nurse, for many years, and I am always amazed at her capacity to give to others. She was divorced a few years ago and hadn't dated much, until she met Rob—a fit and handsome personal trainer—while shopping at a health food store near the beach where she lives. He was there for the weekend with friends, and as they stood in the deli they both felt the instant chemistry and attraction between them. Rob asked her for her phone number, and that evening he called. They had common interests and communication styles, and they talked easily for hours on the telephone. It seemed to Laura that she had met her soul mate.

Laura was sure Rob was the man that she had been waiting for. Within just three months of meeting, Laura and Rob were engaged. Laura had some concerns about Rob's possessive behavior, but she put aside her doubts and immersed herself in love. Within a month of their engagement the trouble began. Rob became quiet and withdrawn. He was often unavailable and secretive about his whereabouts, and then grumpy and defensive when Laura would question him.

Rob lives nearly two hours away from Laura. Rob did not like to drive to Laura's home, so it was she who usually made the trip. When they were together she did most of the cooking and cleaning, and she even mowed his lawn. Because she earns more than Rob, she often helped him with his monthly expenses. Still, she wondered if it was her fault that the relationship was no longer as fun and loving as it had once been.

Soul Mate or Soul Growth?

Laura did not understand why her relationship with Rob was so difficult. She longed for a spiritual partnership, and instead she was engaged to a man who triggered her deepest wounds and fears. She wondered what she was doing wrong.

Laura believed that she was in some way to blame for their problems. She felt that she was meant to be in this relationship and she struggled to understand what her purpose in Rob's life was.

Laura's relationship with Rob also reminded her of her relationships with her father and with her first husband; Rob has the same temperament and controlling mannerisms. Laura found herself reacting to Rob as a defenseless and naïve child. She continued to put effort into pleasing him, but she felt that he was unappreciative and unresponsive to her positive efforts. She did little to take care of herself and soon was weary and tired of trying. She lost what little power she had coming in to the relationship.

Laura tried many times to break free of her relationship. But whenever she tried, she felt overwhelming guilt and stress. Even though the relationship was riddled with problems, Laura felt compelled to stay and try to make it work. The guilt that she felt when she attempted to leave did not make sense to her, yet for a long time she did not make any changes.

Laura's Spirit Guide

From our past sessions I knew that Laura has a spirit guide who calls herself Tess. I know that from Tess's ethereal vantage point she is patiently watching over Laura, trying to help Laura through life's confusion. She had watched Laura give up her power to others many times, and she had watched as Laura detached from her spiritual identity. Tess is devoted to assisting Laura to reclaim her spiritual destiny as an empowered, loving soul.

But this is not so easy; Tess doesn't always feel as if she is able to positively influence Laura. As she felt Laura's confusion and saw her fall back into the pattern of giving away her power to her boyfriend, Tess remained steadfast in her commitment to helping Laura choose to love and take care of herself.

The Drive Home

Laura recently phoned me and wanted to share with me the story of the last weekend that she spent with Rob. She told me that while driving home from Rob's place on Sunday evening, she had begun to replay in her mind their latest conversation.

As she drove she wondered what Rob meant when he said he wasn't sure if she was able to love him in the way that he needed to be loved. In the car Laura rethought her actions and her words, and she wondered if she had been less tired and more fun, then maybe the weekend would have turned out differently. Her anxiety built as she continued driving. Laura thought about how hard she had tried to make this relationship work.

Distraught and trying to understand what to do, she remembered the many times that she has felt the presence of her spirit guide, Tess. She impulsively asked aloud, "Tess, what can I do to make things better? What can I do to make Rob love me?"

After making this request, Laura told me, she felt an instantaneous and strong message to go back to Rob's house. This thought would not go away. She realized that she must go back. She needed to talk to Rob, to ask him how she could let him know she loved him, to tell him that she could not bear to live without him.

Laura took the next freeway exit, made a U-turn, and headed back toward Rob's house. She felt better immediately. Within the hour she turned the corner onto Rob's street, and noticed an unfamiliar car in his driveway. As she entered the house, Laura heard voices and called Rob's name. Amid sounds of confusion, he appeared in the bedroom doorway. He looked at Laura but did not speak, as a half-dressed woman stepped up beside him. Laura said nothing but turned and walked out of the house.

Sitting in her car, Laura sobbed, tears running down her face. She began to realize Rob never really loved her and that she had known this all along. She realized that she had been willing to compromise herself for his attention. She had felt that she needed him, and so he became more important than loving herself.

With a jolt of confidence, Laura made a vow: "I will never, never, ever give my power away to another person. I deserve to be loved and cared for."

Tess transmits love and strength to Laura. She knows how much pain Laura felt at the discovery of Rob's affair. Yet Tess also knows that this is an opportunity for Laura to reclaim her power and begin the process of healing the patterns that created this situation.

Laura's story illustrates the kind of help spirit guides can provide. Tess, in response to Laura's plea for help, sent her the message to turn around and go back to Rob's house. Tess wanted Laura to know the truth of Rob's affair; and even though it was painful, it gave Laura the opportunity to take back her power and learn how to take care of herself in relationships. Laura may have wanted her spirit guide to make Rob love her and bring more positive energy into the relationship.

But the real help that Laura needed was to learn how to love herself.

Meet Your Spirit Guide

It is not always possible to recognize and know your spirit guide in the same way that you know your friends and family. Tuning in to the energy of your spirit guide is a more sensitive and subtle recognition.

The following exercise will give you the opportunity to become more familiar with a spirit guide. Don't worry, you have at least one.

- Find a place in your home where you can relax undisturbed. Lie or sit down in a comfortable position and close your eyes. Take a few deep, relaxing breaths. Inhale cleansing breaths and exhale any stress or tension in the body.

- Continue to breathe and open your heart.

- Send a message to your spirit guide that you would like to connect with his or her energy.

- Imagine a triangle. Notice its color, texture, and any other details.

- Imagine that within this triangle is an image of your spirit guide. If you do not readily see or feel a presence, actively use your imagination to visualize how your guide may appear to you.

- Take a few moments to tune in to the energy of your guide. Pay attention to a presence of warmth, love, and acceptance. Use the skills you learned in the beginning chapters of the book to receive and interpret your impressions.

- Open your eyes when you are ready, and write down everything that you experienced.

If you are an emotional intuitive, pay special attention to any feelings that emerged while doing the exercise. A mental intuitive may have more of a sense of knowing or receive specific information about their guide. For the physical intuitive it is a good idea to tune in to any sensations or gut feelings that come from the solar plexus, the stomach, and the heart area. A spiritual intuitive most likely just needs to trust whatever they receive, as they may experience quite a bit of energy impressions.

Do this exercise often. It will increase your intuitive awareness of your spirit guide. In time you will begin to sense and rely on your spirit guide's presence throughout your day.

22

ASSEMBLE YOUR CELESTIAL LOVE TEAM

~~~~~~~~~~~~~~~~~~~~~~~~~~~~~~~~~~~~~

Rally together your love team of ethereal help. Your angels, spirit guides, and even your loved ones are ready and willing to be part of your love team. All you need to do is ask for their help. They will provide you with steadfast and reliable relationship assistance, twenty-four hours a day, seven days a week.

Their mission and purpose is to assist you in your journey of love while you are here in the physical world. They recognize and immediately respond to your conscious and deliberate desire to connect and communicate with them.

When you open yourself to their celestial help, your angels, guides, and loved ones are given the go-ahead to lovingly influence you and those with whom you are in relationship. They relish your attention and willingness to co-create with them.

Real Love

When I enlisted my spirit guides and angels to help me in love, my relationships became a spiritual-love adventure. Instead of shallow, fairy tale–fantasy types of connections with others, my spirit guides and angels have helped me to embrace the authentic power of love and to feel its source within. We want to believe that it is one's physical appearance, weight, age, salary, and material means that bring one closer to finding and sustaining passionate relationships. Their influence has helped me to detach from these illusions. Love is the glue and substance of the universe, and it is always available to you. Your love team will help you to embrace this truth.

How They Help

Your love team will guide and encourage you in various ways. They will send you sparks of absolute love that will open your heart and give you the confidence to express love to others and the strength to receive it. They will help you become aware of and heal negative emotional patterns that might be keeping you stuck in disappointing relationships. Your love team will draw your soul mate to you and transmit waves of love and harmony into your difficult relationships. They will intensify the passionate love sparks between you and your partner.

Your love team may surprise you by encouraging you to take more emotional risks than you might normally take. You may wake up one morning strangely motivated to confront the fears that have kept you from attracting a soul mate, or you might feel renewed feelings of self-love and self-respect. You may feel a surge of courage and mental clarity that motivates you to sit down with your partner to discuss improving communication or financial concerns. If you are single, you might feel whole, fulfilled, and have a renewed awareness of the love within you.

A client recently told me that she felt that her angels were pushing her and giving her the strength to confront her partner's excessive criticism. She told me that when she talked to him about this, she felt empowered but at the same time had the odd feeling that she was being arrogant. She realized that she had the unconscious belief that taking care of herself meant that she was self-centered and selfish. Her angels helped her to release this belief and move into self-care.

No matter what relationship issue you may be confronting, your love team is here for you.

You Are the Star of Your Life

You might discount ethereal help as distant and ineffective. I have found that this is simply not true. To understand better how your love team helps you, think about the support and assistance behind a successful celebrity performer, politician, or athlete. They might have a manager, an agent, a coach, a speech writer, a producer, and a wardrobe assistant, to name just a few. One person's success is very often dependent on devoted and skilled people who excel in specific areas. All of their talents are necessary to promote the performance and success of the one individual that we view as a "star."

You are the star of your life, and your guides and angels are your skilled and devoted team. The more you ask for their help and recognize and sensitize yourself to their guidance, the more you will shine.

Angels and spirit guides are clever, devoted, and not intimidated by the limitations that we have constructed between the physical and spiritual realms. They see, feel, and know that there is only one world. There is not the physical and the spiritual. We are all one. Let them in, and your love relationships will flourish. They know love.

Assembling Your Love Team

- Find a place in your home where you can relax undisturbed. Lie or sit down in a comfortable position and close your eyes. Take a few deep, relaxing breaths. Inhale cleansing breaths and exhale any stress or tension in the body.

- Continue to breathe and open your heart.

- Send a message to your spirit guides and angels that you would like to enlist their help in co-creating loving, sustaining relationships.

- Imagine a triangle. This triangle is a portal, through which the energy of your love team can come forward.

- If you do not readily see or feel a presence, actively use your imagination and create a vision of your love team. This may be two, three, or more angels and guides; ask them to present themselves one at a time. Do not put too much importance on your ability to visually see them or know their names. This is not as important as we think. Know their presence is real, and in time you will be better able to distinguish their individual characteristics. Pay attention to a presence of warmth, love, and acceptance.

- Send them a question or message. Use the techniques for receiving images, symbols, and interpretation outlined in the beginning of the book.

- Open your eyes when you are ready, and write down everything that you experienced.

Your Love Team by Type

Guidance as Feeling

Emotional intuitives will experience their angels and guides through their emotional-feeling sense. They may experience them as soft, warm, soothing waves of comfort, peace, and gentle protection. Emotional intuitives can be vulnerable in love relationships, often giving more love to others than they expect to receive. Angels and guides can help to correct these imbalances. They can bring the emotional intuitive to understand the importance of self-love and care.

I suggest that emotional intuitives set aside alone time each day to commune quietly with their love team. In these quiet moments, close your eyes, open your heart, and ask your ethereal helpers to fill you with love. Send them your thoughts, concerns, and requests. Open your heart and allow yourself to receive their love and positive influence. Your love team will help you to practice loving yourself unconditionally and instill you with compassion for your perceived shortcomings and inner judgments.

Emotional energy can be a highly charged vibration that directly influences what you attract, create, and experience in your day-to-day life. For this reason it is important that the emotional intuitive reside as much as possible within the positive vibrations of love. They can do this by becoming quickly aware of any negativity, fear, anger, or stress that they may be experiencing, and asking their angels and guides to assist them in processing and transforming these feelings.

Guidance as Knowledge and Truth
The mental intuitive will often experience the ethereal realm through the expansion of consciousness to new levels of truth and awareness. This may be through fresh insights, new perspectives, and the merging of the ego with the greater whole. Mental intuitives can often connect best with their angels and guides by quieting the mind, focusing on the breath, and asking for the truth to be revealed.

Your love team will guide your healing by prodding you to confront negative beliefs and self-sabotaging relationship behaviors. They will often work through synchronicity and by drawing to you the conditions and experiences that will best open you to new understanding of yourself and others.

Mental intuitives can often communicate best with their love team through stream-of-consciousness writing. I recommend that the mental intuitive practice writing down a question or concern, take a few quiet moments of slow breathing, then write nonstop without self-censoring for at least five minutes. With repeated practice, this exercise will provide the avenue for your love team to communicate to you their guidance and advice.

Guidance as Action and Manifestation
The physical intuitive will be most comfortable when the ethereal realm manifests through the natural world. Angels and guides may express their love to physical intuitives through a beloved pet, a persistent bird that seems to watch them, or an early-morning sunrise that opens their heart.

If you are a physical intuitive, your angels and guides will often inspire love activity in physical and tangible ways. This might be by guiding you to be in the "right" place at the "right" time to meet that special person. In times of sadness, they will help to lift your mood by sending love to you through the spontaneous and unexpected helpfulness of a stranger, your dog's excited greeting, or the warm hug of a loved one. They will also often motivate you to express your love in tangible ways to others. Acts of kindness, writing a poem, expressing gratitude to a loved one, and assisting others in need will all help the physical intuitive to feel more love.

Your love team will help you to spiritualize your love. They will motivate you to move out of the more concrete and tangible expressions of love by opening your heart and experiencing love's lofty emanations.

Physical intuitives can ask each member of their love team for a physical memento to symbolize their presence. I myself enjoy doing this. I have a collection of rocks, feathers, gemstones, and other trinkets that my guides and angels have placed in my path to remind me of their presence. I have a small altar where I have placed these objects. They remind me of their love and joyful creative presence. Simply holding these objects will open you to the presence and guidance of your love team.

Guidance as Energy Awareness and Inner Sensitivity
Spiritual intuitives will experience the presence of their love team more directly than the other types. They are more inclined to be able to sense their love team's tangible presence. This might be through "seeing" their angels as wisps of light

and color. They may "hear" them as soft melodies, or whispers of love. In quiet inner meditation and contemplation, spiritual intuitives will be able to tune in to their guides and angels and communicate directly with them. For the spiritual intuitive it is important to trust these connections and stay focused in authentic experiences. Quite often the doubts and disbelief of others will cause spiritual intuitives to question themselves and dismiss what they have truly experienced.

Your love team's desire for you is that you will take the lofty ethereal love, which you know so well, into your physical experience. Your angels and guides will create opportunities for you to express and share your elevated vision of love with others. Spiritual intuitives, please remember that your love team is ready and willing to help you in the material day-to-day experiences of love. No matter how mundane or trivial, do not discount the importance of love experienced in the physical realm.

You Are in Charge

No matter what your intuitive type may be, you can experience and enjoy the communication styles of each type. Practice all of them, as we all have a bit of each type within us.

You will find with a little dedication and practice that your relationship with your love team will become a valued and reliable source of guidance and comfort. Your love team cannot participate in your life without your request. So, remember to ask for help. Be specific and have a clear intent. Your guides and angels will not and cannot take over and direct you in ways that go against your own desires. Your thoughts, actions, feelings, intent, and the direction of your life are up to you.

23

THE INTUITIVE PATH
TO LOVING YOURSELF

L oving yourself deepens the intuition-love connection, as it allows absolute love to flow freely and uninhibitedly through you. Love, in its highest form, is psychic in that it is beyond time, space, and condition. When we flow with love, intuition increases.

One of the most important lessons with which your love team can help you is to learn how to love yourself. You will be loved by another to the degree that you love yourself. Once you unlock the inner treasure of love, it will manifest in your life. If it is your wish to meet your soul mate, you will. If your desire is to heal and improve a current relationship, it will transform—or another, more loving union will come your way. Learning to embrace the love within and to love others often happens simultaneously.

The Inner Love Critic

It can be difficult to love yourself. Even if you have confidence and high self-esteem, you may not always feel compassion and patience for your own perceived shortcomings. Love does not always make sense to the ego-mind. Even if you can convince yourself that you deserve unconditional love, it is usually only temporary. Once you slip up and the inner critic rears its ugly head, you can quickly block whatever love might slip in.

We criticize and judge ourselves based on criteria that our families, our environment, and the cultural consciousness have handed us. Even when we feel worthy of receiving love, we may cling to the barriers that keep love at bay. But love can never really leave. The awareness of its comfort and warmth may slip away like the receding tide, but the great expanse of love will eventually make its way back.

The Shadow of Fear

Love is not an intellectual exercise. It often makes no sense to the logical mind. Fear, instead, makes perfect sense. Things happen and you are hurt, disappointed, or suffer. It happens every day. You see it on the news, in your community, and within your circle of friends and family. It happens to you.

Love is less obvious. It operates not in the things of the world but in energy beyond form. Fear flourishes in the material consciousness; love in the spiritual.

The Love Within

Absolute love lies deep within you. Its source is not your thoughts, emotions, or actions; the source of this love is your soul. The soul is the communal property of the divine. It is more powerful than the ego and the personality-self, the pieces you commonly use to define yourself.

Your soul flows with the current of absolute love. It is interconnected with the beauty and abundance of all of life. It is the pure inner self, where you reside complete and whole. To love yourself, tap into the deep well of love that already exists within you.

Your spirit guides and angels know you as this love, and they can help you to know yourself in this way, too.

Visualization Exercises with Your Love Team

The following two intuitive visualizations will give you the opportunity to experience the love within you and, simultaneously, to become more familiar with your spirit guides and angels.

Metaphors, myths, and fairy tales often open the door to the inner realms of love. These visualizations are presented to you as playful stories that reinforce the intuition-love connection.

A Playful Journey into Absolute Love

The first exercise will take you on a journey to the love planet, Venus. This visualization will help you to release the burden of guilt and shame, and embrace absolute love. With the assistance of spirit guides, you will experience new levels of self-love.

Read through the meditation as you go, or make an audio recording and then listen to it. During the meditation, remember to utilize your intuitive strengths. If you are an emotional intuitive, pay attention to the emotions and feelings that you naturally intuit. If you are a mental intuitive, you may feel guidance coming to you through simple knowing. Quite often, the mental intuitive will experience a large amount of information suddenly and all at once. If this happens, slow down the process and try and integrate what you receive. Physical intuitives may feel shifts and changes in their physical body. Check for tension and stress periodically while doing the meditation. Keep breathing and releasing any stress. Spiritual intuitives may have the easiest time visualizing and sensing their spirit guides. Trust what you experience, and invite all that you intuit into your three-dimensional presence.

Please use your imagination in these meditations and have fun!

To begin, close your eyes and breathe long, deep, cleansing breaths. Imagine on the exhale that you can breathe out any stress or tension anywhere in your body. Continue these cleansing breaths and settle into the rhythm of your natural breathing.

Take a few more long and gentle breaths, in and out, and imagine your heart opening. Visualize your heart as a soft and glowing orb of absolute love. Allow this love to move through you, and as it does it relaxes and softens you. Its warm presence has a life of its own, and though subtle it has tremendous power to expand all through you and to release any energy blocks or resistance to its presence.

Imagine waves of soft purple, lavender, and pink washing over you. A bright golden beam of light touches your heart and gently guides you deeper and deeper into these waves of light and color. The light beam that softly caresses your heart then begins to grow stronger and more brilliant. Your spirit begins to travel within this light beam. You move through the haze and layers of color and energy, and become aware of a large and luminous soft planet. This is Venus, the planet of love, and it is calling and leading you into its radiant glow. You are pulled into its orbit. You can hear strands of chords and musical notes creating harmonious melodies.

You become aware of golden, shining pyramids nestled between fields of flowers and lush vegetation. As you draw closer you become aware of other beings who, instead of physical bodies, have light-energy bodies. Many of them are circling the golden pyramids, becoming more lucid and light-filled as they near the top.

With a strong current of energy, you are immediately transported to the bottom of a pyramid. You feel weighed down as you look at the immense golden pyramid looming over you. You meet a beautiful, translucent spirit guide who has come to welcome and instruct you. She is your love guide. You and your guide are able to communicate without words. Your guide feels what you feel; she is aware of your thoughts, and you and she can effortlessly exchange thoughts and feelings.

Your love guide sends you an image of yourself immersed in pure love. You can see yourself glowing with happiness and joy. In this image you can feel your heart overflowing with compassion, kindness, and unconditional love. In an instant this image of love is transported to the top of the pyramid, far out of your reach. Your guide then sends to you the message that you can integrate and become one with this image when you reach the pyramid's pinnacle. You long for this experience so you search the pyramid for a way to climb to the top. But you are weighted, and it is difficult to move.

Your love guide, sensing your inclination to give up, lets you know that the power of your heart and mind is all you need to levitate and float to the top of the pyramid. You focus and imagine yourself becoming lighter and lighter. You try with all of your effort, but you don't move an inch. Just then, a dragonfly-like creature floats by and asks you to give up your guilt. Your memories and feelings of guilt and shame wash over you, and you envision yourself releasing them. The creature gathers this energy with its wings, and you feel yourself lift off the ground.

Your guide encourages you to go higher. You feel a current of energy move you to another side of the pyramid. On this side the energy is unsettled, and it rocks you back and forth. You begin to feel fears surface; one fear leads to another and then another. The dragonfly-like creature once again comes close, and your guide tells you to release your fears. Without hesitation you let go of all that troubles you. With each fear you release, you become calmer. The troublesome energy current begins to settle down, and you again become lighter and move toward the top of the pyramid.

You are now on the third side of the pyramid. You feel a little lazy and sleepy there. The sounds are soft and the light is soothing; you would like to rest. But you cannot, because your guide interrupts this gentle scene with a push to your solar plexus. The clear message is that it's time to move higher. You are not sure if you want to; this place seems good enough. Maybe you do not deserve what waits for you at the top of the pyramid, and it feels safer to stay in this quiet place. Your guide pushes you again, and you start to feel heavy and burdened.

You begin to move downward, slipping into waves of cool, dull energy. You get the message that you must forgive yourself and others.

You are not sure how to go about forgiving. You let your guide know your confusion and hesitation. Within a moment you feel your heart open and energy move through it. This energy seems to be coming from the pyramid; it is moving through you, opening and stimulating your heart.

You become aware of a pyramid-shaped golden glow within you. Compassion and unconditional love are flowing from it through your entire being. The events of your life—all that you have experienced, said, done, and felt that keeps you from forgiving and loving yourself—come into your awareness.

You can now choose to release these energies; they feel irrelevant, compared with the love and bliss that awaits you. The past, you realize, has no vibrancy or life force. You let go and surrender to the gliding, upward movement.

You feel the support and laughter of your guide as you become a part of a vibrant web of light and energy, which extends from the center of the pyramid.

Your heart, like a star in the sky, is now invisibly connected to the light of the heavens. You glow in this love; you are one with love. You are an active life force immersed in the flow of absolute love.

Empowered with Love

This meditation takes you to Mars, planet of male energy and action. From this exercise you will learn how to feel love as power and how to take care of yourself while loving others.

Close your eyes and begin to breathe long, deep, cleansing breaths. Imagine on the exhale that you can breathe out any stress or tension from your body. Continue these cleansing breaths, and settle into the rhythm of your natural breathing.

Imagine a great wind lifting you; like a hawk, you enter into the stream of the wind's energy, which easily transports you through the atmosphere. As you travel on the wind's current, you see ethereal and translucent colors and shapes. The energy of the wind easily carries you beyond the known and into pure energy. You can feel the soothing vibration of open space moving through you.

You become aware of a dense, fiery red planet looming in the distance. Its magnetic pull quickly draws you into its orbit. A deep quiet greets you as you land on the hard, dense surface of Mars. You feel alone in this desolate landscape, but you begin to explore the large boulders that surround you.

Suddenly there is a deep rumble coming from a large moving mass of rock, and you notice a clear, white light emerging from an opening in the boulders. Like a magnet, you are pulled toward the opening and then down a long underground hallway. As you travel down the hallway, you notice many entrances, and you soon find yourself before a large, golden-red gate.

You hear a voice calling your name, and you enter into a room filled with energy and activity. A male spirit guide greets you with warmth and invites you to relax on a soft, cushioned couch. Immediately, you are relaxed and at peace. You take in the luxury of the room; it is filled with beautiful objects of gold and gemstones. You curiously begin to feel strength and power flow through you. The room fills with people—some familiar, some strangers. They are young and old, male and female, and they are all watching you. You know that you are invincible, as waves of power flow through you. You realize that you have choices in how to use this power. You want to use this power to feel superior and more deserving than the other people in the room.

Feelings of pride swell within you. As your feelings of self-importance and arrogance increase, you begin to experience stress. This soon gives way to feelings of weakness and despair. These feelings intensify and begin to cause more distress. You call out to your spirit guide for help. He is suddenly present and he extends his hand to you. You touch it without thought, thankful that he understands your pain.

Through his touch you begin to feel a different kind of power. This is the power of absolute love. It feels warm and strengthening. Your spirit guide's eyes glow with absolute love and wisdom. You want to feel what he feels, and you communicate that to him telepathically. He nods, and the power that now flows through you is the power of love.

Instead of pride, you now send compassion and love to the people in the room. With each kindness you offer to another, you feel more love and power flow through you. As you share your love, you once again feel confident and self-assured.

You become aware of this love power deep within. And you feel more powerful than ever. The love within you acts like an intuitive radar. It alerts you to the intent and character of the people in this room. This inner radar sends you guidance through thought, feeling, or sensation.

You become aware that some of the people envy you. They sense your love and power, and they want it. They are like you once were. They act in ways that seem loving, but you know that it is not love they feel. You continue to have compassion and love for yourself and for those who feel powerless and unloved. You know that they, too, like you, must find the love that they seek within themselves.

You are kind and loving to yourself and others, and this boosts the energy that surrounds you. You are glowing with light, safe and protected within an aura of powerful love energy. Those who would want to take from you cannot penetrate your light. You know how to take positive, loving actions to take care of yourself, and you send love to these people.

You feel better than you have in a long time. A powerful wind of energy draws you into it. You relax into it. You are quickly transported back to the here and now.

Open to Love Each Day

These story meditations offer a vision of self-love that you can use every day. In doing so you will not only increase your feelings of love, but the conditions, circumstances, and events of your life will respond to love's energy—and you will attract and experience more positive and satisfying relationships.

24

HEAVEN AND EARTH, LOVE AND TRANSFORMATION

~~~~~~

Breathe, open your heart, and accept the love that is available to you right now!

Unconditional love means that no situation—physical or spiritual—can disallow its presence. Love's intelligence and grace supersedes all limitations and conditions. It whispers the eternal truth: that love is always present, everywhere.

Deliberate intuition not only fortifies and enriches your relationships in the here-and-now physical world; it also opens you to the rich and benevolent realm of the divine.

Your Love Quest

Throughout time, humans have sought to experience an intimate connection with the love of the divine. We have gazed into the heavens and sought love's counsel from the stars. We have sung, danced, and prayed to the divine for a touch of love's blessing. The desire to pursue the mystery of the higher states of divine love can be a lifelong pursuit.

In both Eastern and Western religious orders, consecrated monks and nuns commit to lives of devotion, meditation, and prayer to the unseen. In some Roman Catholic traditions, nuns don wedding gowns and wear gold bands on their finger as they take vows committing their lives to the church.

The ancient Greek ritual of *hieros gamos*, or holy wedding, sought to bring the divine presence into the body in order to integrate the physical with the spiritual. Usually practiced in the spring, participants took on the characteristics of the gods through dance and induced trance states. They would then have sexual intercourse, as it was a belief that the coupling of a man or woman with a deity or god would bring spiritual knowledge, love, and blessings of prosperity and abundance.

Divine Love through Relationships

Intimate relationships can also serve as fertile ground for a personal divine encounter. The divine works through the energy of absolute love. When you invoke its presence within a relationship, you are surrendering your personal will to a much greater power. Love has a plan for you. It invites you into a mystery that will refine, purify, and move you and your partner beyond your comfort zones, all in preparation to become whole and one with the eternal soul of love.

The process of transforming relative, ego-based love—the kind of love that we humans are used to—into the lofty unconditional love of the divine is a process that was set in motion at the beginning of time.

These two archetypal patterns of loving, the divine and the human, are best typified through the enduring energies of Jesus and Pan.

Jesus, the Great Lover of the Heavens

Jesus, called the Messiah in some faith traditions, is the great lover of heaven. Jesus had a personal, intimate, and all-encompassing relationship with God, as Spirit. He lived in the physical world, but he never forgot his true home. He was not always comfortable in this world of form and material matter. He spoke of a far greater love and law that transcends the power of the material world. Jesus believed in and relied upon the existence of a spiritual reality in the same way we rely on the physical world. He lived fully in the eternal, in total trust of the invisible Holy Spirit.

In the Bible, the Apostle John tells us that Jesus said, "God is Spirit, and those who worship Him must worship in spirit and in truth" (John 4:24). Jesus taught that there is no greater purpose in this world than to love that which is eternal and without form, and to share that love freely.

Pan

Pan, the Greek god of shepherds and flocks, is a different matter entirely. The son of the gods Hermes and Penelope (or by some accounts Zeus and Hybris), Pan is depicted as a satyr with a reed pipe, a shepherd's crook, and a crown or branch of pine needles. In Greek mythology, satyrs, half-human and half-beast, are woodland and mountain deities.

Pan is the god of nature, the meadows, the forests, and wildlife, as well as human nature. He is also a god of fertility, unbridled sexuality, and carnal desire. In ancient mythology, taking the shape of a goat, Pan chased nymphs through the forests and mountains. During the day he would wander along the mountain peaks and hills, slaughtering wild beasts. At night he played his reed pipes and sang with the nymphs. Legend tells us Pan could often be found in the company of the mother of the gods. Pan loved the earth and all of its material and physical offerings. Even though he was a god, his love was earthly, seductive, and physical.

Into Love's Kingdom

Each of us is caught in the tension between these two mighty forces—the physicality of the earth represented by Pan and the spirituality of the heavens represented by Jesus. Love pulls us into the heavens, into the invisible, and asks us to trust in its intangible truth, and at the same time, the earth seeks love's full expression. It demands our total allegiance to love's rigorous journey. Love on earth is real when it is sensual, forgiving, and transformative.

It is in our relationships that we learn to harmonize the physical and spiritual forces of love. We willingly open our hands and hearts to love's full grace, and each day we are challenged to share and grow, and do the difficult work of transformation.

The Intuitive Divine-Love Challenge

To integrate these two seemingly opposing forces in your relationships is the true work of love. It will require you to put aside your ego desires for self-gratification, and instead allow the mysterious alchemy of love to be your guide. When you surrender control to the divine presence, your defenses will break down, the hold that your ego has over you will weaken, and negative emotions and beliefs will surface in order to be released. This letting go creates an inner space that the enlightened vibration of absolute love will fill.

Each intuitive type will find herself or himself challenged in distinct ways. Emotional intuitives must maneuver their way through the maze of feelings and emotions that are part of every relationship. Their divine task is to not react from fear, distrust, and self-protectiveness, but instead to go within to the purity of love and respond to their partner with compassion, forgiveness, and unconditional love.

It is the ego that is hurt and feels pain. The spirit-self can never be separated from absolute love. It is the emotional intuitive's task to remember to love from this truth.

The mental intuitive's divine challenge is to move out of abstract thought and ideas and become present to another. They must recognize their patterns of belief, thought, and self-interest and move into the divine unknown. This allows them to experience themselves and their partner through the soul eyes of innocence and the beginner's mind.

The physical intuitive is asked to open to vibration, energy, and essence. Their divine task is to spiritualize the body and their desires, and to perceive the soul of another. Their challenge is to open themselves to the flow of divine energy, which they may initially find to be too abstract and nonsensical a concept. It is often only in a relationship that they are able to experience spiritual energy and essence.

Spiritual intuitives come into the state of divine connectedness through sharing themselves fully and completely with another. Spiritual intuitives like to keep a part of themselves private, separate, and at times distant from the messy human world. Paradoxically, it is when they fully immerse themselves and give to another from the depths of their soul that they realize the indestructible power of the divine within them.

Despite your predominant intuitive-love type, you will find yourself confronting all of these challenges. As your intuitive type evolves, all of the four types will begin to strengthen and emerge. This inner integration of the types will empower you not only to master the intuition-love connection but also to fully love another.

Spirit: The Eternal Love

You are doing important work when you love another. Relationships appear to be self-satisfying but they are not. How you love another influences the collective love vibration of the planet and heralds your participation in the great celestial plan.

Each one of us will one day surrender to the heavens and love without form, and when we do our entrance into spirit will be celebrated. You will be cradled and adored by the angels and beings of light for having taken love's journey while on earth. Your pursuit of love will be admired, and your demonstrations of love honored. All of the slights, the suffering, and the misjudgments you may have taken upon yourself as a result of your missteps in loving will be wiped away with a soft laugh, as you pass through the door into love's true kingdom.